Keeping
Your Wife
Your Best Friend

Acknowledgements

My precious Brenda, again I'm in your debt for allowing me to write this book. It couldn't be written without you. The things you do to me and for me keep me falling deeper in love with you. What a tremendous gift from God you are to me!

To my parents, Clarence Sr. and Jerleane Shuler, *thanks* for the example of commitment you set before me. I can't wait to see you again in heaven.

To Christina, Michelle, and Andrea—I pray for your husbands almost daily, that they will be godly men, who love God first and you second. Continue to focus on being God's Best. Remember that God doesn't send His Best to mess.

Thanks to Gary and Karolyn Chapman for EVERYTHING!

"Thanks" to Penny and Gregg Hunter for the idea of the design cover, personal sacrifice and a ton more things you did, exhibiting God's Grace.

Special thanks to Rebekah Lyon for making the cover a reality. Your servant, selfless, Christ-like spirit continues to bless me.

To Steve Wamberg for your ministry to me while editing this book.

To Jerald and Jerra, I couldn't ask for better publishers. I'm so blessed, honored, and humbled to be a part of your *Life Advance* ministry team.

To Bishop Courtney B. McBath for helping me at the *very last* minute.

Thank You, Urban Ministries, Incorporated for the quick turnaround printing for this book.

To Michael and Yvonne Jones: Michael thanks for allowing God to use you in keeping me focused on Him and learning to come to Him with no agenda.

And to all my Prayer Partners whose prayers continue to make an eternal difference!

A very special "Thank You" to our Building Lasting Relationships donors for your prayers and financial support.

Keeping
Your Wife
Your Best Friend

by
Clarence Shuler

Cool Springs Publishing House
Chicago• Colorado Springs

3 5 7 9 10 8 6 4

Keeping Your Wife Your Best Friend
Table of Contents

Foreword

What do real estate baron Donald Trump, TV mogul Ted Turner and former General Electric chief Jack Welch have in common? They are respected and wealthy men who have built business empires. They are also men who have been unable to sustain a marriage relationship for a lifetime. Consider Jack Nicholson, Nicholas Cage and Al Pacino: Oscar winners unable to figure out how to fill the role of committed husband. Ditto for NASCAR's Jeff Gordon. Boxing's Mike Tyson. Tennis's Andre Agassi. All sports champions with marriages that couldn't go the distance. Even "relationship expert" John Gray is on his second marriage.

High profile, highly successful men. But when it comes to being a husband, these men – like so many others – failed. The truth is, I've failed too. I'm still married to my first wife, but in our more than a quarter of a century of living and loving and growing together, I've made a mess of things plenty of times.

Whether you're married for the first time, or trying to get things to work better this time, we're all in need of the same kind of help. We need practical, biblically based guidance if we're ever going to get this right.

Loving one woman for a lifetime in a committed, self-sacrificing relationship may be life's most challenging assignment. It takes hard work. Perseverance. Skill. Wisdom. Grace.

As a husband, you've signed on for one of the most challenging, exciting and rewarding adventures of your life. To do the job well, you need to rely on God's grace and seek out godly wisdom and counsel.

In the pages ahead, you'll find practical insights on how to make your marriage the kind of relationship that honors Christ and brings fulfillment to your life. The author, Clarence Shuler is the kind of mentor you want. He's honest. Real. Transparent. He's made his share of mistakes, just like the rest of us. But when he trips, he gets back up and gets back in the game. He learns from his mistakes and from the rich wisdom he has found in God's word.

So read on. There is hope and help for one of our greatest challenges just ahead.

Bob Lepine
Co-Host, FamilyLife Today

Introduction

Is your wife your best friend?

If your answer is "Yes," you are a blessed man and this book can help you to keep her as your best friend.

If your wife isn't your best friend, but you would like her to be, then this book is for you, too.

What if your wife is already your best friend, but things are not as good between the two of you as they used to be? If you want to rekindle this relationship but you're not sure how, then you may find a few helpful tips in *Keeping Your Wife Your Best Friend*.

Do you remember your first date with your wife? Did you want everything to be just right? Do you remember not being able to think about anything but her? Once she became your girlfriend, you weren't quite as nervous about being with her. The longer the two of you dated, did you become less and less concerned with your appearance as when you were first with her? How about after the wedding and the honeymoon?

It is said that when we're in love, we're not much good for anything. Our minds tend to become an emotional compass focusing on our love of our life, at least at that time. It's difficult to work or study because we're in love!

After the honeymoon, there is a natural tendency to unintentionally begin to take your bride for granted. The reality is that we can't maintain the intensity for more than a few years. But if our marriages are to be forever, then how are we to maintain them through the years after the intensity of the marriage begins to wane?

When I wrote my first marriage book, *Your Wife Can Be Your Best Friend*, I made a simple observation from the numerous marriage seminars Brenda and I had conducted over two decades (not to mention all the pre-marital and marriage counseling). Here it is: *It seems that more than a few men aren't best friends with their wives, even though they want to be.*

It wasn't and still isn't uncommon for men and women not to be best friends when they get married. But other couples *are* best friends when they marry, possibly as high school sweethearts. Then they somehow drift apart. Maybe they allow familiarity, children, or work to drive a wedge between them. The result is a toll on their marriage—and their relationship as best friends.

Others of you may still be caught up in the newness of marriage. Your marriage is so fresh, you still have no clue what happened when you said, "I do." You have no idea of what you have just gotten yourself into. You are beginning a tremendous (and hopefully) life-long adventure! Like most adventures, there are some risks and dangers ahead. Have you gotten "The Look" yet? The Look is a glare from your wife-to-be or wife, that lets you know that you have crossed the line. The adventure is that you may not know that you have crossed the line (and your wife may not tell you—let the mind games begin and they are nothing like dating). This is where the fun begins. Don't panic, you will learn.

Just listen to tennis star Andre Agassi's experience with Steffi Graf, his wife. Andre publicly said (I think this was *before* talking with his wife privately), "If I win the Australian Open (one of the four Grand Slam tennis tournaments), I'm going to get Steffi to play mixed doubles with me." The problem was, Steffi didn't want to play. Not long after his first statement, Andre followed up by telling the press, "It's gone from her looking at me with daggers to 'I'm just going to ignore you for a while.'" (*Tennis*, April 2003, p.24)

Andre experienced The Look. Andre violated Rule #1: *Never commit your wife publicly without discussing the issue privately.*

(Having said that, whatever might cause your wife to give you The Look is Rule #1 at that moment.) This keeps you on the same page with your wife and out of trouble (you *feelin'* me on this?).

I experienced The Look while Brenda and I were engaged. We were at the home of Butch and Rushella Latimer. Brenda stayed with them whenever she came to visit me before we were married. Another friend, James Jones, happened to be at their house. I said something that didn't please Brenda. I really don't remember what I said (a good trait for later years).

Anyway, whatever I said didn't please Brenda. Simultaneously, Butch and James jumped out of their chairs saying in unison, "Did you see The Look?"/" She gave him The Look!" That was my first introduction to The Look. I've seen it quite often over the years.

All men get The Look from their wives. This book may just help you lower the number of looks you get.

Some of you are in difficult marriages, which is no laughing matter. You are in serious trouble, wanting and needing help. Let me encourage you that there is help in this book. I'm asking you not just to work hard, but to work more effectively with your spouse. I can't guarantee it, but I believe your marriage can be restored. If you think your marriage is hopeless, but you want it to work out, then there is a chapter just for you. I believe if you will try some of the suggestions in the chapter *When All Hell Breaks Loose,* your marriage may be saved.

But it's up to you. Sometimes, the changed behavior of one spouse tremendously impacts the other. This influence can be positive or negative. Your marriage didn't get to where it is in one night and it won't be turned around in one night, but it can be restored if you are willing to work consistently and patiently. Some of you have been working hard, and you are not seeing results. I commend you for your hard work, but together let's discover possibly some more effective methods.

What if your wife has mental and physical problems? We'll discuss that too.

Keeping Your Wife Your Best Friend desires to help men with some biblical, practical, measurable, and obtainable marriage principles that will assist those whose spouses may not be their best friends and help those who are best friends to maintain their special friendship.

Pastoral marriages are also included. You may ask: "Why a chapter about pastoral marriages?" Very simply, pastors are human too! Pastors are often excluded because they are supposed to be perfect, thus, they should have perfect marriages. The truth is that male pastors are men, thus, they are human too. So there are pastors who also struggle in their marriages. There is so little written for pastors to assist them in their marriages. I wanted to be sensitive to these men and their marriages.

What if your wife is the pastor? I didn't leave this issue out either. I'm not trying to promote one theological position over another, but dealing with reality in some marriages.

You may not be a pastor, but if you love your pastor and want to support him or her, then your better understanding of the stresses of a pastoral marriage will allow you to offer more effective help to him or her.

As the husband, the man, yes, you are the *head of the house.* What you need to understand, especially from God's perspective, is that "head" translates into "servant leader." This is a foreign concept to many. This book is about serving your wife, not to get more sex, nor to manipulate her; but for the two of you (and your children, if you have any) to experience the best marriage has to offer and what God had in mind when He created the institution of marriage. Hopefully, if you are a Christian, understanding and putting these concepts into practice will even improve your personal relationship with Jesus Christ.

It's this simple: We'll examine, with some depth, some hot topics and real-life examples to help husbands keep their wives as their best friends. Among other subjects, we'll discuss money, sex, pornography, and how to develop a vision for your marriage. This is in no way an exhaustive treatment of these topics, but it should offer a very sound basis for building and enhancing your friendship with your spouse.

Hopefully, you'll also laugh as you read this book. Humor is a part of every healthy marriage, and it's a part of many examples you'll encounter here. The goal is for the case studies and examples to be relevant. I want to communicate to you:

(1) That I know where you live (I'm not saying that I know how you feel because I don't).

(2) That you are not *alone* nor the only one who struggles with your situation.

(3) That you are NOT CRAZY in thinking you can have a better friendship with your wife.

(4) That change is a possibility, which can lead you to a new reality—a better and/or restored marriage.

You will discover as you read the chapters that some thoughts or points will reoccur two or three times. Don't think that the book wasn't edited. The idea is for you to get the point. So if you read something two, three or four times, make a mental note that it's important and you need to understand it.

If you have it all together in your own marriage, maybe you have some friends who are struggling in their marriages. Consider this book as a possible resource for some of those friends, if you like.

Everyone deserves to have their spouse be their best friend from day one of their marriage covenant throughout each day of life they share together. My prayer is that the pages that follow will help husbands and wives alike discover new joy, and enhance their friendships, with their covenant partners.

Clarence Shuler
Colorado Springs, Colorado

Chapter One
Is it Time for a Tune-Up?

Years ago, before earning his doctorate in counseling and while I was single, Don Mann taught me to tune up my 1967 Chrysler New Yorker. Don taught me how to gap spark plugs for that 440 engine by ear! Another guy, Ed Sadler, from our church singles' group, taught me how to change the oil in that car.

This was so much fun because I'm not mechanically inclined at all. My dad used to say, "Boy, you never would have made it during slavery, unless they put you in the house."

Did I mention I'm a little lazy too? I'm not good around the house (this isn't always a bad thing, especially when "Honey Do's" are involved—any ladies reading this, don't tell Brenda I said that). So, amazingly for me, tuning my engine by ear was an exhilarating experience, enabling me to unwind. I never learned these things from my Dad before he died. But it wasn't his fault; I was always too busy playing basketball or too lazy to care.

Changing the oil in my car became rather routine for me. But tell me, how do you know when it is time to change the oil in your car?

Don said that changing the oil, air filter, and spark plugs are the life of an engine. Oil commercials and most mechanics say that a car's oil should be changed every 3,000 miles. I recently interviewed some men who all agreed with the 3,000-mile standard for changing oil. I asked the ones with expensive cars why they changed their oil just like those of us who don't have expensive cars. I guess expense is relative, because most men are proactive regarding their cars.

We've heard about the damage you can do to your engine if you don't change your oil every 3,000 miles. We seem to believe that motor oil television commercial that closed with the mechanic soberly stating, "You can pay me now, or pay me later."

So what about our marriages?

Does Your Marriage Need a Tune-Up or Oil Change?

May I suggest that we husbands need to be even more proactive with our marriages than we are with our cars? Those of us who can't afford to buy a new car or lease one every few years do all we can to make our cars last as long as possible. And those men who can afford to buy or lease new cars every few years tend to take good care of them, too. They want the full trade-in value. I'm not sure that any car was built to last forever, but our marriages are designed by God to do just that: last forever!

(Guys, if you have been married more than once, please trust me, I'm not trying to make you feel guilty. If you have been married more than once, I'd like to help you to make your present marriage your last one, okay? And there *is* a chapter in this book written with you in mind.)

How do you know if your car needs a tune-up? Does your vehicle begin to run rough or begin using more gas than usual? Or are you proactive and take your car to the mechanic before it begins experiencing any problems?

What about your marriage? How can you tell if it needs a tune-up? I don't know about your spouse, but Brenda didn't come with a warranty booklet to inform me just how often she would need a marriage tune-up. Would she need some attention every so many days, months, or years to keep our marriage running smoothly? Would she ever need a tune-up at all?

Let me ask you this: Do you get The Look? Does your lovely bride yell at you and/or the kids? Sometimes—not all the time—her yelling at the children or you could be a result of her perception of her relationship with you. Is she arguing more often? Has she been withholding sex from you? Is she generally less affectionate? All of these could be signs that you need to "take her in for a tune-up."

What Kind of Oil Does Your Car Need?

As soon as synthetic oils became available, I began using them. I believed that type of oil was better and would give a longer life to my engine. Synthetic oil costs more than regular motor oil, but I don't mind spending the extra money. I look at it as a good investment. I want my car to last as long as possible. That's why I do all the scheduled maintenance check-ups and oil changes.

Oil for a car is one thing, but what about your wife? Do you want your marriage to last forever? If your wife needs a tune-up, where do you take her?

With my car, I search out a trustworthy mechanic. I get recommendations, but the mechanic has to earn my trust through several successful repairs on my car. (I don't know too many guys who go to a mechanic who consistently doesn't do a good job on their cars.)

So what about your spouse? Start here: *It takes two to tune-up.* A marriage consists of a couple—a husband and a wife. Both of you may need to go in for the tune-up even if one of you feels you don't need it. And you need to understand, if one of you has a problem, then you both have a problem. It ceases to be her problem and becomes *our* problem. If you don't embrace this principle, then it becomes even more difficult to resolve your marital issues.

Particularly, we husbands may need a tune-up and not even know it. We may inwardly fear such a tune-up: going where we are led to believe few men dare to go—to a pastor, a counselor, or a seminar.

For those of you who are Christians, you can go together to your pastor. Your pastor may refer you to a marriage counselor (in a later chapter, there is a section with suggestions for finding an effective marriage counselor). Brenda and I do marriage counseling because we have found that some couples prefer having a husband and wife team with whom they can discuss their issues.

There are numerous marriage seminars. My favorite would be Dr. Gary Chapman's Toward a Growing Marriage seminar, which is a Friday evening and most of Saturday. Life Advance has a marriage seminar. You could choose Dennis Rainey's *FamilyLife's* marriage conference: *A Weekend to Remember* (Friday-Sunday). Dr. Gary Smalley has a fine marriage seminar. The Billy Graham School of Evangelism has a 75-minute seminar for pastors and spouses on balancing marriage, family and ministry. Many churches have their own marriage seminars. Just listen to local Christian radio or read local Christian newspapers; both usually promote such events.

Even our U.S. Department of Health and Human Services is promoting the Healthy Marriage Initiative around the country. The Initiative's objective is to help people who are married, Christian or not, stay married. Despite what you hear, our government strongly believes the institution of marriage in America is in crisis. Our government has budgeted $1.5 billion to improve the state of marriage, thus, lowering the divorce rate in America. America's greatest threat is the break-up of marriages, not attacks by terrorists. No world power has ever survived the break-up of the institution of marriage and family!

First Things First

Maybe the first thing to do if you are not sure as to whether your marriage needs a tune-up is to *be proactive*. If your car needs a tune-up after so many miles, maybe after a year, no matter how things are between the two of you, suggest going to a marriage conference as a proactive investment in your marriage.

As an option, you could simply spend some quality time together on your own and reflect on your marriage since your honeymoon and wedding. Ask:

- Has anything changed? If so, what?
- What changes have been positive? Why? What can you do to strengthen the positive changes?
- If there have been negative changes, when did you first notice them? Why do you think that these changes bothered you?
- What do you think caused these negative changes? Do you feel that your wife is totally responsible and is being unreasonable, or do you believe that you could have possibly contributed to these negative changes?

If you haven't spoken to your wife about the state of your marriage recently, is there a reason why you haven't?

Maybe You Two Should Talk

Four small words can strike fear in my heart: "We need to talk."

When Brenda says these four words, I'm usually in trouble. These words strike fear in my heart (yours too; admit it!) because they usually signal that something in my behavior needs to change—and Brenda is bringing it to my attention.

It ain't even fun. Sometimes, it is downright *oogly* (that's way past ugly). I tend to get in my defensive posture, while simultaneously trying to act spiritual and mature. I try to appear that I'm ready to discuss the problem in its entirety. Of course, the problem usually seems to be me, or something that I'm doing. (What's up with that anyway?)

If you see or sense things have changed or are changing, why don't you ask your wife if there is something the two of you need to discuss? Sometimes, we don't know how to say what we want to say to our wife. Many times, we don't know how to say it in a way that they can hear it without getting mad at us. Yes, they do the same thing with us, but I'm focusing on our response to them.

Seeing and Remembering The Big Picture

Throughout this book, I will from time to time speak about "The Big Picture." This term implies that marriage is designed to last forever, so I will share all I can to help you make your marriage the *second* best experience of your life (I'll explain later) and for this marriage, if it's your second or more, to be your last.

Your marriage is worth the tune-up, no matter the cost in time or finances. I just had my Jeep Grand Cherokee tuned up. I also had the fuel injector system vacuumed. I'm amazed by the difference in its performance. Before the fuel injector system was vacuumed and I accelerated on a hill, the Jeep really jerked. Now, my automatic transmission smoothly changes from one gear to the other. It also saves gas. My Jeep wasn't in bad shape and I could have lived with the acceleration problem on a hill, but why live with it when I didn't have to?

Remember, a tune-up doesn't necessarily imply that you have a bad marriage. It simply means that you and your wife are smart enough to realize that your marriage is a life-long investment on which you will need to work daily. You're doing all you can to make sure it will last forever, leaving a legacy not only for your children, but also for your grandchildren.

Are you beginning to see The Big Picture? Get a mental picture of how good your marriage can be. If and when things get rough, flash this picture in your mind. Let this picture motivate you to serve your wife. Let it motivate you to work through difficult situations. (Those times will come simply because you and your wife are two different individuals, with gender differences.) As you work through difficulties, it can actually create more intimacy.

Don't let the cost of a marriage conference become an issue, because you are investing in a life-long relationship. Don't let ballgames and computers blind you to what is really crucial: your marriage. Do you remember being able to go out on a date with the woman who is now your wife without caring what was on TV because you just wanted to be with her? Think back and be honest.

Brenda and I will be the first to tell you, after almost twenty years of marriage, that proactive marriage tune-ups are worth it. So whether you're seeing signs that a tune-up is in order or not, take this hint to heart: *A marriage tune-up will keep your wife your best friend—or at least take you one step closer to that goal.*

(This first chapter wasn't so bad, was it? Let's do the questions and hit Chapter Two.)

Action Points
Chapter One
Is It Time for a Tune-Up?

1. Can you tell if your marriage needs a tune-up? How?

2. Are you doing anything to be proactive in regards to a marriage tune-up?

3. Does your wife think your marriage needs a tune-up? Are you afraid to ask her? If you are afraid to ask her, why is this so?

4. Have the two of you talked about each of your perceptions of your marriage? If not, why not?

5. How would you rate your marriage right now? How does she rate your marriage right now? Her rating may be lower than yours, but don't freak (get upset or nervous)—ask why.

6. If your marriage does need an tune-up, exactly what do you think it needs? A good marriage book that your wife and you can read and discuss together? A small group marriage Bible study? A marriage seminar? A biblical marriage counselor, or what?

7. Talk with your spouse about The Big Picture and what it looks like to each of you. What do you want it to be?

Chapter Two
Treat Her Like a Lady

"I can't believe I'm cutting the grass in the middle of the day as hot as it is! This is *not* my idea of having fun."

Instead of mowing the lawn in this sweltering heat, I'd originally planned to be in my nice, cool office writing my next book. My morning schedule was all set. I went to Vince D'Acchioli's *On Target Institute* for men. I did my friendship evangelism by playing tennis with a friend who is on his spiritual journey. I thought that I would come home, spray some weed killer and retreat into the office.

Silly me. When I returned home from my morning responsibilities (Brenda may view them as optional activities), I announced to her that I was ready to spray the yard. Brenda simply said, "Well, the grass *needs* cutting." This statement was accompanied by The Look.

If you've been in a long-term dating relationship, engaged or married, you should know what I'm talking about. You seldom see this Look during early dating or on your honeymoon because your beloved just wants to be with you. She is trying to let you catch her so she can become Mrs. So & So. At this point, she is more focused on getting married, not tweaking you—that comes later. But once you're married, look out! Our wives may never tell us, but they usually nonverbally communicate: "Some things are going to change around here!" with The Look. For you beginners, The Look can be translated: "You need to do this now." Or, "Don't mess with me; I'm serious." Sometimes, it's "You are in tremendous trouble with me and don't even think about sex tonight!"

In this case, it meant "Don't even try to negotiate your way out of this one."

So after receiving The Look, my time set aside to write was immediately exchanged for Brenda's time for me to cut our yard. As I was about to finish cutting the grass, this beautiful Negro—who had so recently pinned me with The Look—came out of the house and asked, "Can you pull the weeds in the window wells of the basement?"

I thought, "I'm not going to get any writing done today. I shouldn't have mentioned anything about the yard and gone to the coffee shop to write." After pulling the weeds, I finally sprayed the yard, which is all I originally had planned to do.

Make a New Plan, Stan

No, I'm not suggesting *Fifty Ways To Leave Your Lover* (your wife). In fact, I'm suggesting a crucial strategy to improve your ability to stay with your lover, your wife.

Why did I change my plans? Have you ever heard the expression, "If Momma ain't happy, ain't nobody happy"? If you haven't heard this expression, you probably will sometime during your married life. And you'll change your plans to accommodate the reality of that saying.

Am I afraid of my wife? No. I willingly chose to change my plans for no other reason than to nonverbally express to Brenda that I love her. It was another opportunity to demonstrate my love for her to her. And after God, she is second in my life with no competition for my love. Was it easy or convenient to demonstrate my love for her at this moment? No. It was very inconvenient, but I love her.

The house and yard are a reflection on the woman of the house. They're evidence as to what kind of housekeeper she is, which somehow translates into want kind of woman she is. Women are inspected by other women all the time. It is a serious trip—it's a "woman thing," but it's so essential that a husband who wants to keep his wife as his best friend must *constantly* be aware of it and properly respond to it. We don't need to understand it, except to know that it is important to our wives. A husband or husband-to-be must pay attention to this critical gender issue, and not to just keep peace in the house (even though peace in the house is a by-product of proper response to his wife's need).

You also need to realize all that your wife does for you, the sacrifices she makes: shopping for the family, daily cooking, washing clothes, taking care of the children, and helping them with their homework. Some wives even give up their careers so that we can pursue ours.

First Class Treatment

A few years ago at Bishop T.D. Jakes' *Man Power Conference*, Bishop Louis Greenup said, "We need to treat our ladies the way we are treated when we fly first class."

He said that he always gets a towel for his wife when she takes a shower. One day, he remembered the little hot towels they give you in first class flight seating before and after you ate a meal. So Bishop Greenup put a towel in the dryer. As his wife was getting out of the shower, he handed her that warm towel. She put the towel around herself and purred, "Hmmm!"

The Bishop took the cue. He jumped in bed repeatedly saying, "Thank you, Jesus! Thank you, Jesus!" I guess he knew his wife was going to thank him as *only* she could.

Bishop Greenup says that he also gives his wife a gift on the day of her birthday and their anniversary each month. The gifts don't have to be expensive, but he wants his wife to know that she is special throughout the year. He went on to say, "The only time some of you men treat your wife special is once a year. That's why *some* of you *get* some (sex) only once a year!"

Little Things Do Matter

Being married for nearly twenty years now, I'm slowly learning that little things *do* matter in keeping your wife as your best friend.

For example, during the first year of our marriage, Brenda had a ritual as I left our two-bedroom apartment. She would ask, "Where are you going and when will you be back?"

I'd have an immediate flashback, thinking, "Didn't I do this drill with my Mom when I was a teenager?" One thing I looked forward to while a teenager was becoming a man: it meant freedom. It meant not having to ask permission from, or answer to, my mother. I thought that when I became a *MAN,* that this phase of my life would be over. Wrong!

But informing Brenda of the details of my whereabouts provided security for her. Suppose I got hurt playing basketball or tennis, or had car problems. She would at least have some idea of where I would be.

This isn't about being henpecked. It's about loving our wives in a way that they feel loved because these little actions say to her, "You are important to me."

Another little thing I learned to do is to call her when I'm going to be late. It is being thoughtful. The call says, "I care about you. I'm putting you first." This is extremely important around any mealtime, **especially** if she prepared the meal.

I also call Brenda when I'm on my way home. Again, it just lets her know where I am. She never asked me to do this, but I think she appreciates it. She can also tell me if she needs me to do something for her while I'm out. This saves gas and time.

We husbands need to do our best Stevie Wonder imitation: we need to "just call to say 'I love you'" to our wives. It doesn't have to be a long conversation. It could be something like this: "Snookums (Pookie, Honey Bun or whatever you call her), I just called to tell you I love you. See you tonight." Such a call lets her know that you are thinking about her. Some husbands call their wives three to five times during the business day.

Men, if we are going to invite someone over for dinner, we *absolutely* need to call our wives to ask if it's okay with her. Sometimes, we forget about Parent/Teacher Association meetings or other schedule conflicts. (Our wives will have those events on their calendars, but we may not have them on ours.) Once your dinner guest is on your wife's calendar, then, you should make this guest's presence at dinner as easy as possible for your wife. Offer to take your guest and family out for dinner, or even bring home Colonel Sanders (the Gospel Bird—chicken). If you don't want to go out for dinner, then why don't you cook dinner for your guest and your wife (and the children, if you have any) or at least offer to help prepare the meal.

Don't *obligate* your wife to cook for your friend and you. But if she *offers* to cook for your invited guest, your dinner guest should see you help in clearing the table and washing dishes (or at least getting those dishes into the dishwasher).

Make the bed occasionally since you both sleep in it. It isn't her job to always have to make the bed. I hate to admit it, but I've just recently (the last few years) started making the bed. You should see the look on Brenda's face when she comes back into the room and sees the bed is made.

I don't know about your wife, but Brenda has all these pillows and teddy bears (she loves bears) on the bed. Keep in mind that all of her bears are to be positioned just so. One day after making the bed, I rearranged her bears. She thought it was so cute and sensitive! I shared this at a marriage seminar with more than *two hundred women* in attendance and they just cooed in *unison*! Guys, I think this is a winner! Men, if we are going to do things our wives like, do them the way she likes them done without offering suggestions for improvement (for example: "Honey, it looks better if you do it this way."). Don't go there.

All these little things continue to demonstrate to your wife your sensitivity to her efforts to keep the family on schedule. These actions birth warm, fuzzy thoughts about you in your beloved's mind. In your wife's heart, she'll know that you love her and that she is extra-special to you. She'll feel secure because your attention to "the little things" will have put to rest any questions about her being in competition with anyone else.

Keep Dating (Keep on Truckin')

Since we're talking about dinner, keep this in mind: When you take your wife out for dinner on one of your dates, remember it is for her. Develop a dating attitude. Remember when you were dating your wife? Weren't you extremely patient and polite just because you were so glad to be with her? Weren't you ready to make that evening special for her just because you were looking for a goodnight kiss, and didn't want anything to spoil it? (Come on, admit it!)

You need that same kind of patience and courtesy when you ask your bride where she wants to go to eat on a date today. If your wife is anything like mine, she'll often say, "Anywhere, dear."

So you'll respond, "How about Chinese?"

She'll answer, "I don't really feel like Chinese."

Then you repeat the question: "So, Honey, where do you want to eat?"

She replies, "Anywhere is fine." You name another place and she doesn't want to go there, either.

Brother, at this point you now realize: "Anywhere" ain't fine. Chill. Don't raise your voice or express your frustration (verbally or non-verbally). Just keep asking until you find out where she really wants to go. Don't get upset. You are doing this for her, with no ulterior motives.

Sometimes, come home and take the entire family out for dinner. Don't forget to call first to make sure she hasn't already cooked dinner.

I don't know about your wife, but Brenda gets tired of planning the meals, so, one week a month with her permission, why not help her plan the meals? (Ask if she wants this help.)

Don't Stop, Don't Ever Stop

Here are a few of the best ideas I've heard (and tried) to let your wife know you care about treating her like a lady:

•Send your wife out for a massage. They aren't that expensive. You can budget for one. Get it as a gift certificate that allows her to schedule the massage whenever she wants to. A good hour massage can be as inexpensive as $40. (Massage students cost less, some as little as $25). *But remember that you are making a love deposit in her love bank, so don't be too cheap.* You want her to feel special. (You can give her one yourself, but don't demand sex because she will think it is the only reason that you gave her the massage. You don't want to ruin a good gesture.)

- On the same day if possible, have the house cleaned
  (or you clean it) or take her to dinner.
- Send the kids anywhere out of the house.
- Cuddle, but don't demand sex. Let her initiate that
  if she wants to. Just enjoy being with her.

A note on that last item: Several years ago, I saw *Waiting to Exhale* as preparation for a radio interview about relationships. If you saw it, do you remember Wesley Snipes meeting Angela Bassett at the hotel bar? They went back to one of their hotel rooms and he just held her all night *without* having sex! More women talk about that scene in that movie it seems more than any other. I'm not suggesting that you need to go see the movie, nor go to the bar to meet a woman, but cuddling our wives all night without sex could be a way of treating them like a first class lady.

I love for Brenda to initiate sex. Not demanding sex, but cuddling makes it easier for our wives to initiate sex. We need to daily touch our wives in non-sexual ways at other times than just when we want sexual intercourse. It is said that the average woman wants to be touched eight to ten times a day in non-sexual way. Don't count. If you have to, don't count aloud or keep a record of hugs on a scrap of paper on your mirror or the refrigerator. We want our wives to feel loved, not used.

Help Your Wife Get Her Groove Back
(Give Her Some Time Off)

Don't put all these principles into practice all at once. The last thing that you want to do is give your wife a heart attack! She will be wondering who it is in your body!

What kills our wives is when we come home and immediately isolate ourselves to watch TV, read the newspaper, or stare at our computer monitor. I understand that you may need to privately debrief or decompress. Just do it before you hit the house. Consider taking the long way home or an extra fifteen minutes in the car before entering your house.

We need to enter our house ready to relieve our wives, especially if they are stay-at-home moms. Our wives feel that they work the day shift, then the evening shift with us watching. To top it off, many feel their husbands want sex as soon as the kids are in bed. It is easy to see how some women might resent a husband who doesn't help out around the house, but wants sex as soon as she has time to rest. So what's a husband to do?

Many wives—mine included—would love for us to help our kids with their homework. I realize that some of you men already do this, which is wonderful. I also realize that for some of us, our kids' homework is beyond us. Helping our kids with their homework is one way of giving her some time off. Helping our girls with their homework is not a good option for them or me, so I'll clean the kitchen while Brenda is helping the girls with their homework. It takes a load off of her knowing that she doesn't have to clean the kitchen too after working with the girls! And the girls get their homework right.

Another option is to send her away for a couple days while you take the kids. She'll love you for it. She needs time to focus only on herself. She usually focuses on everyone else first and then if she has time, she thinks about herself; but she is usually too tired to do anything about it.

Let Her Know You Know

Another way of demonstrating to your wife that you appreciate her is to praise her strengths. It lets your wife know that you notice her abilities, gifts, and talents.

I try to tell Brenda that I appreciate her strengths. For example, she is excellent at keeping our financial records. She is also a more effective communicator than I am. One of Brenda's spiritual gifts is service or helps. She is always offering to keep various women's babies and/or children overnight in order to give a woman a good night's sleep, or to give couples opportunities to have a date night. She has other strengths, but you get the idea.

Brenda's *love language* isn't *words of affirmation* (check out Gary Chapman's *Five Love Languages* by Moody Publishing) as mine is; so Brenda doesn't have to always hear such praise. But she is human, and I think all of us from time to time appreciate and need to hear words of affirmation from our spouse.

Guys, I think our wives are better at this than we are. Let me encourage you to praise your wife's abilities and gifts privately at first. If you do it publicly, and never at home, it may come across as though you are trying to impress others or that you are one way in public and another in private.

If you are praising her at home, then I think it is important, appropriate, and healthy to praise her publicly. It esteems her in front of other women and sets a wonderful example for other men, who may need to begin this practice.

Praising your wife for her strengths keeps your wife from feeling that you take her and her abilities for granted. Your children need to see you do this. Lay a strong foundation for your legacy.

What Do You Think?

Hopefully, you already know your wife well (or at least you're in the process of discovering more about her). I don't think that we will ever know them perfectly, but can you think of some things which would make her feel she has first place in your heart? All the ideas listed are mere suggestions. As you begin to do little things to demonstrate your love and appreciation for your wife, you'll rekindle the flame of romance in your relationship.

Besides, if you love your wife, are any of these things too much to do for someone you love?

Action Points
Chapter Two
Treat Her Like a Lady

1. Are you treating your wife like a lady?

2. Would your wife agree with the answer you just gave? Why or why not?

3. Does your wife feel overworked? Why or why not?

4. Does your wife feel spoiled by you? How do you know?

5. Can you afford to give her some time off? Can you afford not to? What will you, specifically, do to provide that break for her?

6. What little things can you do for your wife to demonstrate your love for her?

7. When can you begin to put the thoughts from these questions into action?

Chapter Three
Before the Fight Begins

"I can't believe Brenda just drove through that yellow light! She knows that I'm trying to follow her to put her van in the shop! I would *never* do that to her if she were following me. I don't know where to go! I don't know where to go; I'm going to get lost if we get separated! She's just assuming that I know how to get to the shop.

"My Daddy taught me how to be considerate when someone is following me. I wish the girls were in the Jeep with me. Then I could tell them, '*That* is not how you drive!'

"Wait 'til we get to the shop. I'll tell *her* about herself and her driving!"

Those were the thoughts that I screamed to myself as Brenda, my beautiful wife, drove through the yellow light ahead of me. Her actions were perfectly legal. The problem was what Brenda's "yellow light move" was doing to me. I was trying to follow her to the transmission shop. Following Brenda at that moment would have taken me through a red light, not legal at all.

What was it about that moment that triggered such a temper tantrum, anyway?

Using My Mental Brakes (What's the Real Issue?)

And what was the real issue? Why was I so mad? An honest and quick re-examination of my heart revealed that I felt Brenda had broken a universal driving law.

You see, my Dad taught me how to drive. He told me if you are leading someone to a particular destination, always make sure that they can make it through the light after you. If they can't follow you through the light, then you immediately pull over, flash your emergency lights and wait for them until they are right behind you again.

I got upset because Brenda didn't do it the *right* way. Or should I say *my* way, the way my Dad taught me. She unknowingly violated my "rights." I'm thinking, "She must not be a good driver because she isn't driving the way I would. Too bad she couldn't have had my Dad for a driving teacher." Those erroneous thoughts were followed by an even more ridiculous notion: "She did it on purpose!"

Why did I get so mad so quickly? Was I tired and still a little frustrated from not being able to fly out of Washington, DC, on Friday evening as planned due to bad weather? Was I tired from playing two tennis matches that morning on a healing ankle? Was I tired from getting only five hours of sleep? Was it just my sin of selfishness—just thinking about me from my perspective?

It really doesn't matter. Regardless the case, I had no acceptable excuse. I was wrong!

Rethinking My Position

What happens to you when your anger toward your beloved spouse hits the boiling point—at no fault of your spouse? Lately, this is what happens to me: All of a sudden, as my temper and self-righteousness is rising, a thought (I'm sure planted by the Holy Spirit) occurs to me. *What is Brenda's perspective on this situation?*

Usually, when I go off like I did trying to follow Brenda to the transmission shop that day, I don't think that anyone has the right to a different perspective. There can be only one perspective: *mine!*

That being said, Brenda's perspective may actually have complimented me that day. Say what? Brenda constantly says that I never forget where places are. She has always been amazed by the fact that I can usually remember where a place is if I have been there only once, even if it's been years since we have been to that place. So maybe, she assumed that day that I remembered where the transmission shop was, even though it had been almost a year since our van was there.

Or maybe Brenda thought, "We both have our cell phones. If we are separated, we can call each other." That's logical enough, isn't it?

Or could it be that she was trying to save time because she had to cook dinner and we had a parents' meeting at the high school shortly afterwards?

Resolve Problems Before They Get Worse: They Won't Just Go Away

If you want to keep peace in your marriage and not carry the additional weight of bitterness, then read the two following Bible verses. Even if you don't believe in the Bible, these principles will help you. (However, I believe you may need the power of the Holy Spirit, given only to Christians, in order to put these principles consistently into practice.)

First Corinthians 13:5 says, "Love keeps no record of wrongs." **What?** This verse says that I am not to keep a record of the number of times, from my perspective or in reality, that Brenda wrongs me? How do I do that? Dr. Gary Chapman says that we should keep short accounts, not letting disagreements go unresolved more than a day or two. As a couple, we certainly need to discuss with our spouse when we feel that we have been wronged.

Sometimes, our spouses will do something to us and we will just let it go for awhile. We say to ourselves, "I'm not going to bring that up." The problem develops when we don't forget about it. We begin keeping an account of the wrongs our spouse does to us. What inevitably happens is that our spouse will do something that upsets us and then, we let them have it! You let her know what a good spouse you have been by not telling her the things she has been doing wrong. And to support your point, you now tell her all the things she has done which offended you. This illustrates how a spouse can keep a record of the wrongs of their spouse. You think you haven't gotten mad until now. If that's the case, then why are you are getting even?

Ephesians 4:26 reads, "In your anger do not sin; do not let the sun go down while you are still angry." Isn't it good to know that being angry isn't a sin? Yet we have to be careful not to let our anger *move* us to sin. "Not letting the sun go down" while we are angry with our spouse is being proactive. If we don't reconcile with our spouse before the next day, what usually happens? For most couples, it just gets worse. Some people think that if they don't talk about their problems, their problems will just go away.

I don't think so.

When we don't discuss our problems and go to bed, Satan speaks to our minds. He'll tell me when I'm mad at Brenda, "You *know* she did that on purpose. She's testing your manhood. Put her in her place. Doesn't the Bible state that you are the head of the house?"

At the same time the enemy will say to Brenda, "How many times do you have to remind Clarence about that? He keeps doing that on purpose! He doesn't respect you."

Wrestling with these types of thoughts all night will not bring you closer to your spouse in the morning. More than likely, they will make you even more upset. .

You have to realize that your spouse isn't the enemy. Your spouse is on the same team with you, remember? Resolving conflict may require that one individual make a personal sacrifice for the good of the couple. The couple has to ask, "What is best for us as a couple?" This answer should be the guiding factor for the couple.

Brenda and I have a vow from our wedding: We will not go to bed angry. Over the years, this has meant some very late nights (yes, even early mornings) before we go to bed. It's been worth it. We now keep extremely short accounts with each other. We still pray about it before talking to each other about problems. We also look for the best time for our spouse to receive. Is our spouse tired or can they give us their undivided attention? Can *we* give *them* our undivided attention? We're open for each other to share additional concerns. We try to be careful about not only what we say, but also how we say it.

If you are wondering if I have ever broken this vow, the answer is, "Yes." But it has been less than five times in almost twenty years of marriage.

Another consideration is that your wife or you may need more time to process a conflict. Your wife or you may say, "I can't forgive you right now." The response to that should be, "When can you forgive me?" Brenda and I recommend no more than two days be taken for a spouse to forgive the other. This method provides sensitivity to your wife's or your emotional make-up, yet does not let either of you let your emotions go unchecked with no time limit. This way, the spouse who is more emotional knows that at the end of the two days (one is better), he/she is going to have to reconcile. This rule needs to be agreed upon before disagreements are in progress.

One Less Egg to Fry

As we got closer to the transmission shop, Brenda almost made the wrong turn. She corrected herself before I needed to contact her, but she was right. I did remember exactly where the transmission shop was!

I was angry for nothing. The bottom line is this: Had we argued, I would have not only lost the argument, but also hurt Brenda in the process. Thanks to the Holy Spirit's pushing me to try seeing this situation from her perspective, an unnecessary fight was avoided. In fact, this situation drew me closer to her and makes it easier to ask the question: Why does what Brenda did bother me so much? It doesn't mean never questioning Brenda about her actions, but trying to be fair about it and attempting to evaluate my motives before speaking to her.

I believe the Holy Spirit tries to talk to me more than I realize. This particular day, I heard Him. I think I was in position to hear Him. I think, the more time spent with Him, the easier it is for us to hear and respond to Him. What do you think? Are you spending time with God, so you can hear Him when he speaks to you?

Value Her, She's Worth It

Later in the evening on the same day of the "yellow light offense," I was sitting in a principal's meeting with her and some other parents. Brenda often attends these meetings without me, but I decided to go to be with her. I'm the girls' parent too.

It was the height of summer, a few weeks before school began. Brenda got up and came back with a cold bottle of water for me. I didn't ask for the water, but it was so hot in the library where we met that night. The air was stifling, and the cold water revived my tired spirit as it went down my throat.

Here was my best friend, sensing a need and meeting it because she loves me. Now you need to know that she would have done it regardless of whether we'd argued or not that afternoon. That's the way she is. But this water tasted much better because we hadn't argued earlier that day.

Looking at things from Brenda's perspective is the right thing to do because I plan to spend the rest of my life with her and our relationship is priceless! I have to remember that and not take her for granted or think, consciously or subconsciously, that God put her here to wait on me hand and foot because I'm the *Man*.

Is It Worth Going to War Over?

I'm not suggesting that you should never disagree—and sometimes strongly—with your wife about certain issues. I am suggesting, however, that you choose these battles carefully. You need to ask this question, "Is this issue worth going to war over?" I think you'll discover that most things aren't.

I realize that this may be confusing to some because how can you keep a short account and still express a healthy and necessary point of conflict? Keeping a short account is easy. Once things are resolved, don't hold onto them or keep bringing them up. Mentally, train yourself to be in control of your emotions and not controlled by them.

In order to still participate in healthy conflict, remember that conflict is natural. But examine your motivation for conflict: Is it to wound, to heal, or for clarification? What is best for your spouse, you, and both of you as a couple? It may be wise to answer these questions before proceeding further into the conflict.

In my book, *Your Wife Can Be Your Best Friend*, in chapter two, *She Changed after I Said "I Do,"* I give nine steps you should consider in handling your disagreements.
Here they are:

•Agree that your goal is to gain mutual understanding, not to win the fight.

•Pray aloud and together. This is difficult when you're in the heat of battle, and it requires humility and submission to God. Thank God for each other and for the opportunity this difficulty provides (James 1:2- 4) for you to learn more about each other and to trust God more.

•Define, agree to, and stick to the real issue. Don't let past offenses ooze into the argument. Keep to the issue at hand.

•Don't mimic each other. Don't say, "You said…," then mimic the tone of the voice your spouse used.

•Don't call each other names or use fighting words, like, "Yo Momma." You know your spouse's hot buttons. Words like, "You always," "You never," or labeling like "You're lazy," or "You don't care," just incite. Don't go there. Stay in the safe zone by stating how you feel or what you perceive, but don't manipulate.

•Don't yell or raise your voice or hand to your spouse.

•Outline your rules ahead of time. One person gets to state what he or she is concerned about and actually gets to finish his or her statement. Then, the other spouse gets to offer a "rebuttal" or answer without interruption. Then each spouse should summarize what he or she has heard/ understood the other person to say/feel.

•Pray after you've reached an understanding. Ask God to help you leave this argument with Him. Don't take up an old offense, but forgive as He has forgiven you. Thank Him for something you've learned about your spouse.

•Reestablish your bond with your spouse by hugging and/
or holding hands. It's helpful if you can do this even
during the argument. It reminds you of the closeness you
should have as a couple, and that the goal is biblical
oneness and understanding.

I'm concerned that some of our disagreements may be
unnecessary. They can often be avoided if we can slow
ourselves down and first evaluate our own motives as to why
something bothers us so much. Then we can see if our
concern is legitimate, or just selfishness.

Seeing the Big Picture

About one hundred years ago—actually, in the early
1970s—I played basketball for Moody Bible Institute. Our
team ran a two-guard offense with no point guard. The other
guard, Dave, averaged 23 points per game. I averaged 17
points per game as a first semester senior.

Our team, the *Moody Blues,* scored almost a hundred
points a game—and this was *before* the three-point shot (I told
you it was a hundred years ago). We had seven players scoring
in double figures. Life was good. All I thought about when I
got the ball was shooting. My coach had given me the green
light, so when I saw orange (had the basketball), I fired!

Unfortunately, my personal focus on basketball and
dating was out of balance. I neglected my studies, resulting in
my flunking out of Moody.

After getting my grades up, I transferred to another
Christian college in the NAIA to play basketball. My new
coach told me that I'd never be a scorer in this new league.
He said that I needed to learn how to play point guard. (I
wish he would have told me that when he was recruiting

me—I turned down a walk-on scholarship to Wake Forest University to go to a Christian college.).

I had no clue how to play a point guard. I sat on the bench that year behind one of the best point guards that I've ever seen, Leroy Higgins. It took about a year, but Leroy taught me how to be a point guard.

The average fan usually doesn't appreciate those players who don't score much, but after I left this Christian school, being a point guard turned out to be a blessing in disguise. My experience as a point guard enabled me to make a basketball team that traveled to Brazil to play. I could play on summer league teams with former Atlantic Coast Conference basketball players, the best of the best.

What's the difference between the shooting guard and the point guard? The shooting guard's responsibility is to shoot the ball when he or she gets it; the point guard is the coach on the floor. The point guard has to see everyone on the floor, keep everyone motivated and set the tempo, which is best for his or her team. It is a much more rewarding position because it involves the entire team and not just yourself. It is a position of leadership and service.

Adopting a point guard mentality with our wives will help us keep them as our best friends. We need to become students of our wives. What makes them tick? How do they mentally process? Do we communicate from their perspective? Do we serve them? This is what a point guard attitude in marriage produces. If we learn how to do this, we can stop arguments before they even begin.

This type of perspective is essential to servant leadership, which is what Christ does for us. It isn't flashy. It certainly isn't self-promoting. But it is one essential strategy in keeping the "home team" healthy.

Your wife deserves no less.

Action Points
Chapter Three
Before the Fight Begins

1. When is the most recent time you have gotten frustrated with your wife? When was the last time you "went off" on her and you were wrong? (If you think you have never been wrong, maybe you're not being honest with yourself.)

2. What was it about?

3. Did you express your frustration to your wife? How did you do it?

4. Do you regret even sharing the frustration? If you needed to tell her of your concerns, do you regret how you expressed your frustration?

5. When you have been wrong about a shared frustration with you wife, how did you feel? Why? (Write it out for your sake—don't just bury it.)

6. When you are frustrated with your wife, does she still know that you love her and feel loved? Does she know and feel that you love her but may not approve of her actions? (Depending on where your relationship is, you may want to discuss this point.)

7. How do you make up with your wife? Do you do the same things: flowers, dinner, and a movie? Think of doing something you have never done. (Ask her mom or her friends for ideas if you need to.) Consider praying with your wife as your first step in making up.

Chapter Four
Show Her the Money

Remember in the *Jerry McGuire* movie when Cuba
Gooding, the football player in this movie, says to his agent
(played by Tom Cruise) "Show me the money?" As a professional football player, he wants the biggest contract he can
get because the average career of a pro football player is only
four years, not forever.

Few of us are professional athletes earning their amazing
salaries! Most of us (and justifiably so) are concerned about
our finances, especially with the uncertainty of our economy
the last few years. According to the non-profit organization
FamilyLife's research, financial security is one of the five basic
needs of most women. This isn't to imply that women are
greedy, selfish, or insecure. It seems that it is just a part of
most women's (certainly not all) nature or make-up. Just like
for most men, certainly not all, sex is number one among a
man's five most basic needs.

Yet, money is one of the top five reasons married couples
divorce.

It seems natural for most men to want and expect to
provide financially for our spouses. After all, our fathers and
grandfathers drilled that into us. That being said, is it so
surprising that many of today's women *don't* feel this way?
This critical difference in perspective needs closer
examination.

First Peter 5:8 says, "If anyone does not provide for his
relatives, and especially his immediate family, he has denied
the faith and is worse than an unbeliever." (Some Bible
translations of this verse call the man who doesn't financially
provide for his family a *fool* or an *infidel*.) As the head of the

house, and the perceived primary provider, it is probably safe to say that most men feel they should also manage the financial books for the household. This responsibility is often assumed as head of the house's role.

Remember, when this verse was written it was the man who was the primary earner for the family. There was no need for a welfare system because men were to provide not only for their immediate family, but also for other relatives. But the verse doesn't say who is to keep the financial books.

Who Should Keep the Books?

For generations, men kept the financial records for their households. Women were actually considered not intelligent enough to have this responsibility. Today we know that such thinking was erroneous. But sadly enough, even in this day and age, it is still not uncommon for a man to die leaving his wife without a clue regarding their financial situation. Such a household is living in the past.

Today is quite different. More and more women share in the breadwinning, working outside of the home. Women who work outside the home desire to have, and tend to have, a more active role in financial management at home. Yet all women work hard, especially mothers. A new attitude that recognizes this reality is also giving at-home mothers and wives a more active role in how the money in the home is managed.

So who should keep the financial records? *How about the one who can effectively do the family accounting and has the time to do it?* During one of our marriage seminars, after Brenda's session on *Money in Marriage*, a woman came up to Brenda crying. She sobbed to Brenda, "I keep our financial records. I have a drawer full of bills. If my husband knew how much in debt we are, he'd leave me!"

Brenda gave her some ideas to consider. One suggestion was for the woman to pray about telling her husband about their situation. Brenda felt it was better for her to tell her husband about their finances than for him to find out from a collection agency by mail or an impersonal phone call. There would be no easy way, which the woman was praying for, to tell her husband. After a few months, Brenda received a phone call from this woman. The caller was praising God because she told her husband and to her relief, he didn't leave her, hit her, or look down on her. But he did begin managing their finances again. Their marriage is doing better because they are doing a better job of communicating. Their lack of communication about their finances had been the beginning of their problem.

At one of our more recent marriage seminars in Norfolk, Virginia, one man made a commitment to keeping his wife informed about their financial status, even about spending thirty dollars. (This isn't for everybody!) A year later, his commitment paid off. He and his wife have a blossoming relationship. She feels more love because he is including her more in their financial planning. This simple action provides her a greater sense of security—both emotionally and financially. Her trust in him is at an all time high in their marriage. This husband actually created more intimacy with his wife by allowing her involvement in managing their money together.

When Brenda and I got married in July of 1985, she had just earned her Masters of Religious Education from seminary. She hadn't had the opportunity to get a job. Did I mention that she was also planning our wedding? So Brenda was a little busy in the spring of 1985.

Having graduated two years earlier from the same graduate school, I was the only one with a job and I kept the books. I had to keep them when I was single, so I didn't give it a second thought when I got married. It never entered my mind for her to be in charge of our finances. It wasn't that I thought Brenda was dumb. I just never thought about it at all and I don't remember her asking.

Initially, I had no problems keeping the books. I was thirty-one years old when we married and had been living on my own for quite some time.

Five years into our marriage, I changed jobs. I felt called to start a church. I actually should have started it about three years earlier, but that's another story. The demands of a family with twin baby girls with one on the way and starting a church from scratch were incredible! It took more time than I could have ever imagined.

One day when I arrived home, Brenda showed me a red cutoff notice for a bill that I hadn't paid. It was the last cutoff notice. If I didn't pay it that very day, our electricity would be cut off by nightfall. It was 4:00 p.m. I had to drive downtown and pay the bill before 5:00 or the electricity would be no more. It would be seriously *chilly* in the house, but not just because the electricity wasn't on, if you can catch my drift.

Without nagging or disrespecting my manhood, Brenda asked if I wanted her to start keeping the books since I had so many things to do. I silently laughed to myself, reassuring myself that I could do it all. After all, I was the *Man*.

Didn't my wife know she'd married Superman? This late bill was just an oversight, an isolated one-time incident. It wouldn't happen again. I simply told Brenda, "Thanks, but I can do it. I was just exceptionally busy the last two weeks, but thanks for offering to help."

Unfortunately for Brenda, I'm a slow learner. It wasn't the last time this situation occurred. It actually happened two more times. Each time, Brenda offered to begin keeping the books if I wanted her to. The third time, Brenda's offer didn't seem quite so ridiculous as it did the first time. For one thing, I was getting tired of racing downtown to pay a late bill. (This was before the days of the Internet and online payments.)

Another issue for my consideration was how Brenda felt. We always entered our house through our garage, never through the front door. These cutoff notices were always put on the front door. That meant the only way that the cutoff notice could be brought to Brenda's attention was when someone rang the front doorbell. Then, surprise! Brenda saw the cutoff notice for the first time in front of a friend or better yet, a stranger. How embarrassing this must have been for Brenda, who never complained once during the three times this happened to her!

What was the problem? Why was I beginning to be consistently late in paying the utility bills? We had the money in the bank. We weren't living check to check. So what was the deal?

Well, my home office has never been the neatest corner of the universe. I organize with piles. Bills were not exempt from my strategic piling, either. So I'd get the bill, place it on my desk, and somehow, a pile of paper grew over it. Out of sight and out of mind—and the next thing I knew, I was racing downtown to avoid having one of our utilities off.

For the third time, Brenda asked if she could take over keeping our financial records. She knew I was simply too busy. My messy desk didn't help me. She didn't say any of that; she just said, "This is one less thing that you have to worry about and I have plenty of time to do it."

Now, as I gave over the books to Brenda, that didn't relieve me of my responsibility to know what was going on financially in our household. And even more important, it was critical to communicate to Brenda that she was not responsible for making the money to pay the bills. Often if the woman is keeping the books and she doesn't work outside of the home, she can't help but see the financial needs and often feels that making a contribution to the financial aspect of the marriage is her responsibility. This may put all kinds of stress on your wife, which she may never communicate to you. Therefore, you need to tell her that she is just keeping the books and you will make the money.

Even in our household, Brenda works part-time for *Pampered Chef*, but we don't factor that into our family budget.

What's Your Family Financial Vision?

If you're asking "What's a family financial vision?" then you'll probably find this section to be one of the most critical in the book for you.

If you are in debt, let me encourage you to develop a plan with your spouse to get out of debt. Getting out of debt *is* possible, but it takes a lot of sacrifice (denying yourself), consistency and patience. There are numerous non-profit credit companies whose sole purpose is to help people get out of financial debt free of charge (if you go this route, always check the company with Better Business Bureau).

I'm grateful to my father-in-law, George Stokes, who taught Brenda to be financially prudent. Because of Brenda, the only bills that are constant for us are our house payment, car insurance, and groceries. No matter how much or how little we make, we don't live check to check. All it takes is a little discipline. For example, Brenda uses coupons for our groceries and other items. She has trained our girls not to ask her to buy certain cereals unless we have a coupon for them.

I can't tell you the number of young and new brides that Brenda has helped save money by using coupons. She has even helped those whose household income is six figures to save money. Why give your money away unnecessarily?

We also pay all of our credit card bills on time. We don't accumulate credit card debt. Credit card interest can run as high as twenty-eight percent these days. We believe in using credit cards that benefit us, such as an airline credit card or a credit card that pays you money back for using it.

If you do have credit card debt and you want to pay it off more quickly, write two checks to the company and mail them back together. One is your regular payment and the other should be marked *"principal only."* If you don't write "principal only" on the second check, the credit company will apply the extra money as a regular payment split between your interest and the principal. So they get paid and continue charging you interest. It's all legal, and most credit card companies won't tell you this. So if you are sending an extra amount of money in each month to pay down your debt, but see little or no improvement, this is why.

Not only do you need a financial plan for getting out of debt and for staying out of debt; but you also need a financial legacy for your children and their children. You don't need to make your children millionaires, but you need to be prudent enough so (at the very least) they don't have to deal with your debts when you've passed on to glory.

On the Same Financial Page

While serving as pastor of a church, our elders and I were made aware of a financial need for someone in the church. Don Kentner, one of our elders, said he thought that he and his wife could meet the financial need in order to keep the church from taking on an extra burden from its budget. Then he made this statement: "Before I can write a check, I need to check with Shelley (his wife). We have an agreement that we have a limit as to how much money we can spend without talking about it with each other."

I was shocked! I didn't think he was henpecked. I was shocked because I had never heard such an idea before. It was, and is, so profound! The more I thought about Don's statement, the more I liked it. I was so captivated by Don and Shelley's financial principle that I told Brenda about it. She loved it too. We agreed to adopt their principle and are still using it.

We've shared their financial principles with couples literally around the world. The response is always the same. What a wonderful idea! It is a built-in marriage financial accountability system.

Maybe you and your wife should consider adopting Don and Shelley's principle.

Who Should Make the Money?

In our culture today, I'm not sure it matters who has the greater income if you and your wife work outside the home. I do think that if your wife makes more money than you that you need to be able to deal with it. Be glad you have such a gifted wife.

I met a couple where the wife was smarter than the husband. So she naturally secured a higher paying job. Try as he could, this husband who made an exceptional salary was never going to make more money than his wife. She loved him and was totally devoted to him. To her, it was no big deal. But he couldn't handle it. I think he let it play with his warped idea of manhood. They eventually got divorced. I always felt this was the reason. They had two children. It was sad and could have been avoided.

Brenda is smarter than me. We both have our master's degrees. I would love for her to work outside the home. I'm sure she could earn more money. I can cook (don't tell her) and I can get the girls off to school. Man, I could play tennis every day. I'm *ready* to be Mr. Mom.

I think what is crucial is for the couple to realize that no matter who earns the most money, the money is *theirs*. They are on the same team and shouldn't be in competition with each other. You as a couple need to decide what is best for you in the marriage's money management department.

Let me encourage you to have several savings accounts where you don't withdraw the money. Consider developing an education (for children), vacation, date, car (for maintenance and a new car or a newer used car), and emergency accounts along with your other financial accounts.

When you purchase a newer used car (unless it is a Lexus or something like that) you allow someone else to pay for the depreciation. Even after your car is paid for, keep paying into the account. That way when your car needs to be replaced, you have a substantial amount for a down payment. Even if you only put this money in a bank account, it is still drawing interest. A substantial down payment gives you more leverage with car dealers and more options.

You work hard for your money, let your money work hard for you!

Whose Money Is It Anyway?

Psalm 50:9-12 reads, "I (God) have no need of a bull from your stall or of goats from your pens, for every animal of the forest is mine, and the cattle on a thousand hills. I know every bird in the mountains, and the creatures of the field are mine. If I were hungry I would not tell you, for the world is mine, and all that is in it."

Colossians 1:15-17 states, "He (Christ) is the image of the invisible God, the firstborn over all creation. For by Him all things were created: things in heaven and on earth, visible and invisible, whether thrones or powers or rulers or authorities; all things were created by Him and for Him. He is before all things, and in Him all things hold together." These verses clearly state that everything, including people and money, were created by God. So it all belongs to God and He is just letting us use His things. We are simply stewards of His possessions.

For those of us who are Christians, our first financial obligation is to worship our Lord and Savior Jesus Christ through our financial giving. God asks those who profess in Him to give ten percent, a practice called *tithing*. We can't repay God, but tithing is a way of first, obeying Him; secondly, demonstrating our faith in Him; and thirdly, praising God. I also call it "spiritual investing."

In the Bible, when the master gives to his servants, he expects his servants to multiply what he gives them. To those that do, he gives more. The more that is given, the more that is expected. But to those that don't produce, often that which is given is taken away and given to someone who will multiply it.

Most people want to be rich, but most are not faithful with what they already have. If they are not faithful with a little, God is not going to trust them with a lot (read the Parable of the Talents—Matthew 25:14-30). It is not that God loves them any less; it's simply a question of stewardship. You don't keep loaning money to a friend who never pays you back. You don't stop loving them or spending time with them. In fact, you treat them as though they don't owe you money, but you don't give them any more money until they repay you. You don't want to contribute to their dysfunction.

What's It All About?

Money is neutral, but our response to it can make it beneficial or detrimental. It is critical that we own money and not let money own us. Many of us feel we never have enough money. We may have more than we need. Try living below your means, not living check to check. (That's not really living is it?) As Americans, we are much richer than citizens of many other countries. Having traveled overseas so many years, I agree with the rest of the world about our wealth.

The money you and your spouse earn, if she works outside the home, can be used to bless numerous people:
•your children if you have any,
•their children,
•your church,
•others in ministry,
•friends in need, and
•organizations and causes near to your heart
    and God's purposes.

As we deal with money, we must force ourselves to see The Big Picture. The key is how you manage the resources God has given you. The question is, "What kind of financial legacy will you leave?"

Action Points
Chapter Four
Show Her the Money

1. Who keeps the financial records in your home? How did you come to that decision? How does your wife feel about this decision? Why?

2. Do you have a vision for your family finances? Why or why not? If you don't, why don't you consider setting aside some time during the next weekend with your wife and begin to do some futuristic financial planning? Sometimes, it is difficult for our wives to follow us if we don't have a vision or we are leading them nowhere.

3. If you and your wife don't have a family budget, create one as soon as possible. Start now by listing the items you think should be in that budget, and how much you need to budget for each one.

4. If you and your wife work outside the home, who makes the most money? If your wife is making more, how are you handling this? If it bothers you, how does your wife feel about the way you are dealing with this situation? If you are struggling with this, can you talk with your wife about it? If not, why not?

5. Are you in debt? Do you have a plan to get out? Are you living check to check? If so, what can you do to break the cycle? Consider using coupons for groceries and generic brands instead of name brand food and clothes, etc. You can save a lot of money this way.

6. If you are a Christian, are you giving God what is His? Are you worshiping God, not just with your words and song, but also with your finances?

Chapter Five
It Was Good for Me; Was It Good for You?

Sex is one of the greatest gifts God has given to men and women. Unfortunately, if misused, sex can be one of men and women's greatest stumbling blocks.

Maybe that's why discussing sex can often be awkward. But it can be especially awkward for those of us who grew up in homes where our parents never talked to us about sex—or, worse, if there was sexual abuse.

Yet Dr. Howard Hendricks of Dallas Seminary says, "We should not be ashamed to discuss what God was not ashamed to create."

Can You Woo Woo Woo?

Some years ago, Jeffery Osborne released the song, *Can You Woo Woo Woo?* It caught on quickly and women loved it. I think women loved it so much because this song spoke of romance—specifically, of the man romancing his woman.

Guys, our women still want romance. Romance is an expression of our love for them. It is more than buying flowers and taking our wives to dinner. Romance is our love-motivated actions for our wives that fills them with warm thoughts, often transforming their entire being with feelings so that she desires to give herself to the man of her dreams—you. Our romancing our wives says, "I care about you and you are worth more than I can ever give you."

Romance demonstrates to our wives that we love them for who they are and not just for their bodies. Even though you may have been married for many years, your wife still wants to know that you love her. In fact, most wives still thrill to hear us say, "I love you."

I know some of you men are saying to yourself, "She knows I love her. I told her I loved when we got married. If it changes, I'll let her know." You, especially, need to read on.

Keep Dating Her

Continuing to date your wife should become a permanent aspect of your marriage. Get your wife and both of your calendars so the two of you can schedule a date. A regular date night is good if your schedule allows for it. Make your dating and your sexual intimacy a priority. Brenda and I recommend twice a month and at the very least, once a month. You're investing not only in your marriage, but also in the marriages of your children and grandchildren. Your marriage actions will affect the legacy of your family. Your children will see your dating as natural and plan on doing it when they get married. All work and no playing with your wife will damage your marriage.

Once you make the date, don't break it. Don't just talk to your wife about becoming more romantic. In fact, that may be the worst thing you can do, especially if you have told her this before. Let her see you being romantic.

Budget for your romance, for your monthly dating, and for weekend getaways. (If you are a pastor and your church can afford it, arrange for them to send you and your wife away for a few days during *Pastor's Appreciation Month* in October). Make sure if you do decide to budget financially for dating and other romantic adventures to include your wife in the process. Then, the two of you pray and agree about the amount of money you will set aside for investing in this aspect of your life. She may lose "that loving feelin'" immediately if the two of you aren't on the same page regarding the amount you set aside for your romance.

Don't surprise her when it comes to finances. Remember that one of you is likely a spender and the other is a saver. Don't let what could be an excellent idea to improve your compatibility to be used by Satan to become a source of conflict between the two of you.

If you are struggling with being romantic, go to www.familylife.com and look up *Simply Romantic Nights*. Your wife will love you for it. Take her on weekend retreats three or four times a year if possible.

Have you heard the expression that you have to get women in the mood and men just have to be in the room? I think there is some truth to this cliché. I used to always wonder why the format for the date was usually flowers, romantic movie and/or dinner in a restaurant with style and then a man could usually look for a kiss at the end of the date.

Women tend to be holistic. How they are treated all day affects them, whereas most men are compartmentalized. What and how we communicate to our wives can stay with them all day. Whereas, we men can fight with our wives one minute and want to have sex the next.

Your Wife's Sexual Perspective

Here is a Dear Abby article you may find funny at first. Yet it may be disturbing the more you think about it. The title of the column is, *"Honey, Was It Good for You?"*

Dear Abby,
I have been waiting years to see a letter, like the one from B in Dallas. She said she faked orgasms. I'm glad to know I'm not the only woman who does this. Now, I feel less like a freak. Please print all the letters you can get on this subject.
Faker

Dear Faker,
I could not believe the volume of mail. Read on.

Dear Abby,
Of course, I fake it. All women do, I adore my husband but he could not find my erogenous zone with a road map, so I go through the motions to keep from hurting his masculine ego.
Deserves an Academy Award

Dear Abby,
Most of men have the rabbit habit—hop on, hop off. Athletes know that in order to perform well, they must warm up first, perform and then cool down. The act of making love is no different. If men followed these instructions, women wouldn't have to fake it.
The Midwest Coach

Here are a few more samples:

Dear Abby,
My darling is 65 and he is making and I'm 63 and still faking it. When I read about these men who are still active at 85, I *shudder*, I don't think I can survive another 20 years of this. Dear God, don't they ever wear out?

Dear Abby,
Married 22 years, been faking it for 20.

Dear Abby,
I fake it just to get it over with. Sex was never as important to me as it is to my husband, but it is so good for his ego, I'd

never let on that all my wild carry on was an act. We have been married for 44 years. He is faithful and so am I and ours is a loving, solid marriage.

Initially, these women's comments may appear comical, but when given more thought, these comments are heartbreaking. In the last comment, this woman says that she has a good marriage, but she is missing out on sexual pleasure. One has to question how good her marriage is if she can't tell her husband about her sexual frustration. Would his anger go out of control? Maybe she has tried to tell him unsuccessfully.

In all of these situations, the problem is that the husband doesn't know what it means to serve his wife and meet her needs in a sexual way. These men are clueless. Are you?

Dr. Gary Chapman gives suggestions for husbands and wives to improve their sex life in his book, *Toward A Growing Marriage*. Here are a few, from the ladies first and then the men.

From the Ladies:

1. Show more affection, attention throughout the day; come in after work and kiss my neck.
2. Spend more time in foreplay; love, play, and romantic remarks are important
3. Try sex at other times than at night when I'm tired.
4. Write love notes occasionally; send homemade love cards.
5. Try not to ejaculate so soon.
6. Do not seem as though you are bored with me in the evening.
7. Take more responsibility for getting the children settled so I can relax and share more of the evening with you.

From the Men:

1. Be attractive at bedtime—no hair rollers. Wear something besides granny gowns and pajamas.
2. Be aggressive occasionally.
3. Do not always be on a time schedule that places sex when we are both physically tired.
4. Do not try to fake enjoyment.
5. Do things to catch my attention; a man is easily excited by sight.
6. Allow variety in the time for sexual act (not always at night).
7. Do not allow yourself to remain upset over everyday events that go wrong.

During a FamilyLife Marriage Conference sexual intimacy talk, you will hear that passion is fired through planning, unselfishness (or generosity), and creativity.

Sexual Intimacy: A Biblical Priority

"²But since there is so much immorality, each man should have his own wife, and each woman her own husband. ³The husband should fulfill his *marital* duty to his wife, and likewise the wife to her husband. ⁴The wife's body does not belong to her alone but also to her husband. In the same way, the husband's body does not belong to him alone but also to his wife. ⁵Do not deprive each other except for mutual consent and for a time, so that you may devote yourselves to prayer. Then *come together* again so that Satan will not tempt you because of your lack of self-control."

1 Corinthians 7:2-5

Paul of the New Testament is often called a chauvinist, but if you closely examine his teachings, you see this isn't the truth.

Verse two in the above passage is an example of gender equality in the Bible, especially considering that the culture of the day didn't observe women's rights. But God does give women equality and rights. The instructions given in verses three and four are that the man and woman are to fulfill their sexual responsibility to each other. The Christian husband and wife are also informed that their bodies don't belong to them, but to their spouse. Understanding and applying verse five is crucial to any marriage. According to the Bible, no Christian couple should deprive each other of sexual intercourse unless they both agree to do so for the purpose of prayer. They are also told to have sex as soon as this devoted time of prayer is over so that neither will be tempted by Satan and a lack of self-control.

So fighting fair in marriage includes not withholding sexual pleasure from your spouse.

Men, be careful not to abuse this passage of Scripture. Don't demand that your wife have sex with you. Yes, the Bible does say that your body is not your own because it belongs to your spouse. But biblical love is about voluntary giving. For women, how they are treated outside of the bed is just as vital an aspect of sexual intimacy as the physical act.

Yes, you and your wife are to have sex on a regular basis, but I believe that it is the man's responsibility as the spiritual and servant leader to create a climate where his wife wants to voluntarily give herself to him for his pleasure. In like manner, the husband should want to give himself to his wife for her pleasure.

Guys, we need to get in shape so we can have longer physical endurance in our lovemaking. This results in pleasure for our wives. It is no fun for her if it is over for us and she is just getting warmed up.

Another practical example of making sex a priority comes from the wisdom Brenda heard from a friend. Brenda and this older woman had been trying to have lunch for almost a month. They finally found an open date in both of their schedules. The day they were to have lunch, the older woman called Brenda to cancel with virtually no explanation.

The older woman hesitated, then finally told Brenda in a somewhat awkward voice. She said, "Brenda, my husband has been gone for a week. He is very energetic. Well, when he comes home tonight, he will want to have sex and I just have to have a nap, so I can be rested and ready for him." She understands the biblical priority of sex. Her response is motivated by her love for her husband, not fear of a demanding or overbearing husband.

Can My Sex Life Get Better?

What do you do if you were a virgin until you got married and your sexual experience isn't as incredible as you thought it would be? First and foremost, don't blame your spouse.

Our preconceived notions about sex might provide us with an open mind. On the other hand, they may actually hinder our ability to physically enjoy and express our love for our spouse.

You may have unrealistic expectations if your knowledge of sex has been overly influenced by our culture's view of sex as seen on TV, at the movies, and on videos. As the man, the world's culture focuses on the man's pleasure. Sadly, the woman is just a tool for man's pleasure. It also focuses on the man, pardon my expression, being the *stud*. You know, *Don*

Juan, James Bond, Bruce Lee, Shaft and their buddies are the heroes from which we derive our male sex models. I admit I enjoy watching these movies. But a problem is created if we look to these guys to model how to woo a woman. (And if we are *real* men, our wives after sex will become putty in our hands, longing to fulfill our every beck and call. Yeah, right!)

A critical first step toward a more satisfying sex life may be healing yourself from your past. It isn't uncommon for couples to enter marriage with different and unknown expectations regarding sex. Our parents, knowingly or unknowingly, laid the foundation for our expectations about sex. However, the influence of others also plays into the picture.

At the marriage conferences that Brenda and I conduct, I sometimes ask attendees how many of them were taught about sex by their parents. The percentage is usually less than 15%. More than 60% learned about sex from their peers. There's no doubt about it: Our expectations and knowledge are influenced by who has taught us about sex.

My parents taught me about sex when I was 15 years old. This was back in the sixties when you could be in high school and still not really know anything about sex.

My parents educated me in 10-15 seconds. My Mom said, with my Dad sitting beside her, "Boy, keep your *thing* in your pants and your pants zipped."

That was it. No more discussion. I don't know how my parents expected me to learn about sex. I guess they figured when I got married, I would learn then.

Let me be fair to my parents, however. They were concerned for my safety and so called my conduct into accountability. I had been asked by a faculty member of Wake Forest University, who was white, to take his daughter and her cheerleader friend to a concert. This was in the late sixties in

Winston-Salem, North Carolina and race relations weren't the best. My entire family met to determine if I could go or not.

Love Her and Her Body

Another possible hindrance to romance and tremendous sex could be our insensitivity to our wife's body. All of our bodies change as we get older. Our wives' bodies sometimes change, especially after having children. They may have stretch marks; their breasts may begin to sag.

Some women are unable to regain the figure they had before children. Unfortunately, some husbands actually demand that their wives lose the weight gained since they have been married, regardless of the reason(s) for the weight gain. Some wives may experience difficulty in losing weight. When their wives can't lose this weight, they often feel unloved and/or guilty, which can lead to depression. This insensitivity can be interpreted as not loving their body, and thus, not loving them.

This can begin to cause our wives to stop feeling attractive. If our wife doesn't feel attractive, then she has a difficult time believing that her husband finds her attractive. In fact, she may think to herself, "What's the use of dressing nicely since he feels I'm unattractive anyway?" She may then begin to dress in an unappealing manner because this is how she feels. She may also think, but may never express to her husband, "If my husband doesn't find me attractive, then why does he want to have sex with me except for getting a physical release?"

And, as the song says, "What do you do after the love is gone?" If our wives feel this way, then they can feel like a prostitute whenever you do have sex.

Therefore guys, don't criticize your wife if she gains weight which she never loses. We married for better and for worse. She is still the wonderful person you married. Don't criticize her for her stretch marks or for drooping breasts. Some of us have changed too! I'm going bald and weigh some thirty-five pounds more now than when Brenda and I got married. Some of us have gained weight and we didn't give birth to any children. Some of us are losing our hair.

If you want your wife to lose weight because it is healthy, then offer to exercise with her. Pray about this first as to how to say it, if to say it at all, and when to say it. Our neighbors, a couple who lives across the street, go walking everyday. Not only are they exercising together, they get to talk everyday.

The bottom line: Compliment your wife and her body.

What If Your Wife Wants Better Sex?

Suppose your wife does what Brenda did to me? As I was driving, Brenda asked me, "What do you think about our sex life?"

Don't do what I did at that moment. Man, I freaked! I thought, "What was she doing asking me what I thought about our sex life? Is she implying that she is not being satisfied? This was messing with my manhood, and I'm a black man too! Aren't all black men supposed to be studs?"

I didn't know what to do, so naturally, I quickly changed the subject. I didn't respond like a godly man should. In fact, I got defensive.

When Brenda asked me this question, she wasn't mad. She wasn't complaining. In fact, she was being brave, willing to discuss such a personal issue with a guy who is highly emotional. So if you ever hear the question from your wife, don't get defensive. Don't take it as a shot to your manhood. Just listen. Hear each other, then discuss it. After you have heard and understood each other, then pray about it.

Next, I would recommend immediately beginning to implement these new adjustments. What started out as a threat may result in your experiencing an incredible treat!

If You Wake Her, Go the Distance

Have you ever heard your wife's head hit her pillow with a noise that simultaneously sounds like a groan and moan. She's worn out from her day. Often the last thing she wants to do is have sex. She's TIRED!

You may have had thoughts of sex tonight, anyway. What do you do?

Let me make three suggestions. First of all, let her SLEEP! Go to sleep without sex tonight! What a great example of servant leadership. What a practical gift of love to your wife. She'll love you for it. Such a demonstration makes it easier for her to follow your leadership.

The last thing she needs at the end of a difficult day is the additional emotional baggage of guilt, feeling that she let you down or that she isn't the perfect wife. You don't want your wife just going through the motions sexually. You both want passion. You can't have passion if one of you is tired. Serve by letting her know that you are thinking of her by not demanding sex. Why don't you give her a massage, with no other agenda? A wife once told me that her husband de-manded sex every night. That couple is now divorced.

Secondly, help your wife around the house. By lightening her load, you are helping her to have more energy. You are communicating to her that you love her. Last year in the Shuler household, one school morning we all left the kitchen in a mess. Brenda and I had separate all-day responsibilities outside of the house that day. She and I had agreed to give counsel to a woman with marital problems (I don't counsel women alone—it's a safety barrier).

I got home about an hour before Brenda. This was just enough time to prepare for the counseling session. As I looked at the kitchen, I realized that Brenda would have a fit if any woman saw her kitchen the way it was.

I had a choice to make. I could prepare for a counseling session or demonstrate my love for Brenda. I chose to clean the kitchen, which meant going into a counseling session unprepared. The biblical priorities are God first, Brenda second, my three girls third, and the ministry fourth.

You should have seen Brenda's face as she came in the door at the same time as the woman we were to counsel. Brenda was making excuses why the kitchen wasn't clean. Then Brenda saw the kitchen. Her eyes found me and radiated her love for me. God supplied the wisdom for counseling the lady.

That night, Brenda rewarded me as we enjoyed each other's body. My cleaning the kitchen was not motivated with the idea of having sex that night. The motivation was my love for Brenda, not for sex. Brenda initiated the sex; I graciously received it. I didn't want Brenda to miss her blessing. Indeed, "It is more blessed to give than to receive."

Thirdly, if you wake your wife up at night, you need to be able to go the *distance*. By going the distance, I mean give her pleasure. A quickie here won't do. You know that men and woman respond differently to sex. It usually takes women longer to get excited. Try to bring her to orgasm. You can do this by stimulating her clitoris gently with your finger. If you get tired, change fingers. Give her pleasure first, and then you can experience pleasure because it doesn't take you as long to reach orgasm.

If you wake her from her sleep after she is so tired, you *really* need to make it worth her while. Put a smile on her face and a memory in her mind.

Lastly, there is no place for physical abuse. Brenda and I speak for *FamilyLife's A Weekend to Remember* marriage conference. The speakers are always critiqued so we can improve. I used to joke about Brenda hitting me with her right hand and snapping her wrist (a boxing term). The feedback I received from several women stated that my jokes weren't funny because their husbands were physically beating them. I no longer joke about physical abuse.

Sadly, I was counseling by phone a woman and friend who lived in another state. She told me that she was divorcing her husband. She worked on a church staff and he taught Sunday School. She said something that I've never forgotten: "I don't want the hands that beat me one moment caressing me the next." Her husband was demanding sex every night, never considering her feelings, and physically abusing her.

When Quickies Are Okay

Quickies are okay, as long as you and your wife are doing well in your relationship. Quickies can't be the main menu in your sexual relationship. Quickies can open the door for spontaneity and be a shot in the arm for your relationship. For quickies, if your wife is a stay-at-home mom, get a babysitter and enjoy lunch at home or away from the house. If your wife works outside of the home, go to her office with flowers and take her to lunch—maybe even at your house.

Oral Sex

Some biblical scholars believe that the language in the Song of Solomon is symbolic. For example, in the Song of Solomon, the authors of *Intimate Issues* (p.181) believe Solomon's genitals are called fruit in 2:3 and his bride's genitals are called her garden in 4:12-16. So 2:3. "And his fruit is sweet to my taste," 4:16, "Let my lover come into his garden and taste its choice fruits," and 5:1, "I have come into my garden, my sister, my bride," are just a few of the references to oral sex.

Say some romantic words to your spouse. If you can't think of words on your own, use the Song of Solomon.

For the men, use 7:1.
> "How beautiful your sandaled feet, O prince's daughter!
> Your graceful legs are like jewels,
>   the work of a craftsman's hands.
> Your navel is a rounded goblet that never lacks blended wine.
> Your waist is a mound of wheat
>   (guys, don't go here: stay out of trouble) encircled by lilies.
> Your breasts are like two fawns, twins of a gazelle.
> Your neck is like an ivory tower.
> Your eyes are the pools of Hesbon
>   by the gate of Bath Rabbim.
> Your nose is like the tower of Lebanon
>   looking back toward Damascus. (I wouldn't go here either.)
> Your head crowns you like Mount Carmel.
> Your hair is like royal tapestry:
>   the king is held captive by its tresses.
> How beautiful you are and how pleasing, O love,
>   with your delights!
> Your stature is like that of the palm,
>   and your breasts like clusters of fruit.
> I said, "I will climb the palm tree; I will take hold of its fruit."
> (Have mercy!! This is hot and in the Bible too!! Smokin'!)

For the ladies use 5:10:
> "My lover is radiant and ruddy,
>   outstanding among ten thousand.
> His head is purest gold; his hair is wavy and black as a raven.
> His eyes are like doves by the water streams, washed in milk,
>   mounted like jewels.

His cheeks are like beds of spice yielding perfume.
His lips are like lilies dripping with myrrh.
His arms are rods of gold set with chrysolite.
His body is like polished ivory decorated with sapphires.
His legs are pillars of marble set on bases of pure gold.
His appearance is like Lebanon, choice as its cedars.
His mouth is sweetness itself; he is altogether lovely.
This is my lover, this is my *friend*, O daughters of Jerusalem.

Whether you believe that oral sex is appropriate or inappropriate, communicate with your spouse so you both know what each one of you is comfortable with. Biblical love is about giving and serving, not taking or forcing. The attitudes of giving and serving should be present before, during and after sexual intimacy. Love is not demanding. So spouses, don't demand that your spouse give you oral sex. Pray about it and create a climate for trust and self-giving. If your spouse isn't comfortable with oral sex, then live without it.

Remember, incredible sex doesn't make an incredible marriage, but *incredible* marriages should have *incredible* sex!

Questions for Thought
Chapter Five
It Was Good for Me: Was It Good for You?

1. How did you learn about sex? Did your parents educate you or did your peers? Did they do a good job? Why or why not?

2. Did what you learned from them help or hinder your sexual relationship with your wife? Why do you think their information helped or hindered you?

3. How would you describe your sex life: unsatisfactory, satisfactory, incredible? Why?

4. How would your wife rate her sex life: unsatisfactory, satisfactory, incredible? Why?

5. Are you having sex as much as you would like during the week?

6. Have your wife and you talked with each other recently about your sexual relationship and/or satisfaction?

7. Are you comfortable talking with your wife about your sexual intimacy? Why or why not?

8. Are you still romancing, dating, and complimenting your wife and her body? Why or why not?

9. If you and/or your wife want to improve your sex life can you and your wife discuss it? Why or why not?

10. Remember love is not demanding, but giving. Consider creating an environment in which your wife loves giving herself to you. What do you think it would take for that to happen?

Chapter Six
When All Hell Breaks Loose

Four years ago, my first marriage book (and my second book in all), *Your Wife Can Be Your Best Friend*, had just been published. I was so excited, thinking, "I'm becoming an author!"

I gave a copy to one of my local prayer partners. He got the book and raced through the table of contents. He dejectedly, yet gently put my book aside on his coffee table and complained, "When is someone going to write about how to stay in a marriage when all hell breaks loose, like it has in my marriage? I'm catching hell."

My initial, selfish thoughts were sad because he wasn't excited about *my* book, but I had to agree with him that my book was incomplete because I didn't touch that topic. He was right. I should have written about this subject, but it never crossed my mind because I wasn't experiencing his kind of difficulty.

He didn't know about Gary Chapman or Gary Smalley. Both have written about going from defeat to gaining victory in tough marriages. They have written entire books on this subject. I briefly want to give you a few things to think about if you are in a marriage that you wish you could make better—or leave behind.

What You May Already Know: But Don't Blow Me Off!

If you're a Christian and you feel all hell has broken loose in your marriage, you probably know most of what I'm going to say. But it won't hurt you to hear it again. Besides, I may say some things of which you may not be aware.

Take a look 1 Corinthians 7:12: "If any brother (Christian man) has a wife who is not a believer and she is willing to live with him, he must not divorce her." The verse doesn't say if they are getting along. Quite possibly, they may have many arguments because one is a Christian and one is not. Often the Christian, who has the best of intentions, may create tension by trying to force his/her mate to become a Christian by preaching all the time instead of modeling the consistent Christian life before the non-believing spouse.

Verse fifteen of this same chapter says, "But if the unbeliever leaves, let him do so. A believing man or woman is bound in such circumstances; God has called you to live in peace. How do you know, wife, whether you will save your husband? Or, how do you know, husband, whether you will save your wife?"

So it seems that one ground for divorce is desertion by the unbeliever. God allows separation for Christians, but the goal of the separation is for the couple's reconciliation (vvs.10-11). God desires for the Christian spouse to be a catalyst or vehicle for his/her spouse to develop a personal relationship with Jesus Christ.

Matthew 19:3-9

> Some of the Pharisees came to Him to test Him. They asked, "Is it lawful for a man to divorce his wife for any and every reason?" Haven't you read, He replied, "that at the beginning the Creator 'made them male and female,' and said, 'For this reason a man will leave his father and mother and be united to his wife, and the two will become one flesh? So they are no longer two, but one. Therefore, what God has joined together, let man not separate.'" "Why then,"

they asked, "did Moses command that a man give his wife a certificate of divorce and send her away?" Jesus replied, "Moses permitted you to divorce your wives because your hearts were hard. But it was not this way from the beginning. I tell you that anyone who divorces his wife, *except for marital unfaithfulness (adultery)*, and marries another woman commits adultery."

After reading Matthew's passage coupled with the Corinthians passage, you can see that God grants only two grounds for divorce: adultery or you have a non-Christian spouse who leaves you. That's it! Most couples that divorce should have done more investment and investigation before they got married.

What You Need to Believe

The first truth you need to believe is that God does love you and has an incredible plan for your life, if you will obey Him. Read Jeremiah 29:11, "For I know the plans I have for you," declares the Lord, "plans to prosper you and not to harm you, plans to give you hope and a future." God's promise is made to God's people of which you are one if you are a Christian. We can say the application of this verse is the same for an individual Christian as well as for the entire Body of Christ. You may already know John 3:16 by memory. It speaks of, "For God so loved the world…" Put your name in place of the world. GOD SO LOVES YOU!

For the next truth, listen to Psalm 37:4: "Delight yourself in the Lord and He will give you the *desires* of your heart." Matthew 6:33, "But seek *first* His kingdom of God and *all these things* will be given to you as well." I believe "the desires of your heart" and "all these things" include your marriage. These two verses are conditional, however. *If* you put God first, *then* these things will happen in God's time, which isn't always the same as our time.

To be honest with you, God's timing and mine usually aren't even close. I want things done yesterday and He's trying to teach me to live by faith, by having me wait for His perfect timing. The truth these two verses reveal is *the necessity of putting God first and everything else after Him.*

God's sovereignty is the next truth that you need to embrace. Look at Psalm 121:3, 5: "He will not let your foot slip—He who watches over you will not slumber; The Lord watches over you—the Lord is your shade at your right hand." There are numerous verses in the Old and New Testament demonstrating God's sovereignty and His incredible love for you and me.

The woman to whom you are now married is the one with whom God wants you to experience all His blessings. No, God didn't make a mistake. God created and loves the institution of marriage. The one to whom you are now married is the one to whom He wants you to stay married, too!

Staying in a Difficult Marriage

The grass may appear to be greener or may actually be greener on the other side of the fence or lot, but remember, it still will need fertilizing, watering, cutting, and aerating. In other words, don't fantasize yourself into a divorce. If you divorce your wife, and go into another relationship, you will still have to work at the new marriage. In fact, you may have to work harder because of your baggage from your previous marriage, which often sabotages the new marriage (usually, unintentionally). And that is why when people divorce, it is usually a first step toward their third marriage.

God loves divorcees, but He hates divorce. Divorce attacks marriage, the institution God created and loves. Malachi 2:15, 16, "Has not the Lord made them one? In flesh and spirit they are His. And why one? Because He was seeking godly offspring. So guard yourself in your spirit, and do not break faith with the wife of your youth. 'I hate divorce,' says the Lord God of Israel, and 'I hate a man's covering himself with violence as well as with his garment,' say the Lord Almighty. So guard yourself in your spirit, and do not break faith.'"

In *Your Wife Can Be Your Best Friend,* I go into tremendous detail to explain why divorce may not be your best option. I'm not judging or condemning anyone who has been, or is, divorced. My sister is divorced and is doing a super job of raising her two children. (I often try to get her to trade her children for mine, but she won't.)

Divorce statistics reveal that once divorced, the odds are 90% the divorcee will get remarried and 80% divorced again. And then, you will get married again. So a divorce for most Americans—certainly not for all, but for most—is usually the first step toward being married three times.

When it comes to divorce, the heart of God is about grace and forgiveness. Let's think about Hosea 3:1: "The Lord said to me, 'Go show your love to your wife again, though she is loved by another and is an *adulteress.* Love her as the Lord loves the Israelites, though they turn to other gods and love the sacred raisin cakes.'" In the Old Testament, if a woman was found guilty of adultery, the husband by law could have her stoned (and not with marijuana). Hosea is demonstrating grace, forgiveness and love to his wife, which Christ has done for all of us.

You Can't Change Her... but God Can Change You

This you know because if you could change her, you would have by now. I definitely would have changed Brenda by now if I could. Since you can't change her and your efforts to may cause her frustration, quit trying to change her. Don't quit the marriage, but do quit the tweaking.

I imagine some of you are reading this section and are saying to yourself, "I'm not the problem, she is." I hear you, but look for a moment at The Big Picture.

A couple of years ago, I was the speaker at a men's retreat. After one of the sessions a man approached me for help with his problem. The first thing he told me was that he and his wife hadn't been sexually intimate in almost a year! I'd started silently praying for wisdom when he approached, but after that opener I became intense in my prayer. His pastor joined us. This successful lawyer went on to tell us that his wife had stopped attending church and wouldn't let their sons attend church.

I knew we had to get more information. We had to unlock the key to his and her past. The lawyer told us that his wife's father had sexually molested her and one of her sisters. Another sister threatened to report him. In response, the father threatened to put her in an insane asylum, but he never touched her.

What was really bothering the lawyer's wife was that her father had recently asked Jesus Christ to come into his life and forgive his sins. He was becoming an elder in another church, and she believed the church was wrong to put her father in leadership. She had lumped all churches together, which was why she stopped attending church. She knew God would forgive her father of his sin, but she felt he had "gotten away" with what he had done. He had never apologized to her or her sister for his sexual sins against them. She was also angry with her mother for not stopping her father.

The other daughter her father had molested eventually married, but was now divorced. The daughter who threatened to report him hated men and had vowed never to marry. Yet another daughter was headed toward divorce and possible mental breakdown.

My first thought of theological wisdom in response to what I had heard was, "Wow! How do I get out of here?" First, we all prayed for God to intervene in all the lives affected. Next, I told the lawyer that God may want to use him to unite this dysfunctional Christian family. I asked him if he could get his wife to agree with God that she needed to forgive her father. This wasn't necessarily to build a bond between his wife and her father. Rather, it was to release her from being in emotional slavery to her father, which was impacting her as a Christian, wife, and mother.

I suggested that the lawyer have his wife write a letter to her father, which she would never give him. In this letter, she would tell him exactly how she felt and why she felt that way. After she wrote the letter, she would tear it up and start another letter, devoid of some of her emotion and written in such a way that he would want to respond. At that time, the lawyer didn't think his wife would agree to this part of the task.

Then I suggested that the lawyer begin to pray for his wife's father. The goal was for God to move the man to ask his daughter for forgiveness for what he had done to his daughters. I committed, along with others with whom he shared, to pray for him and situation.

Six months later, I returned to this church to participate in an ordination service of a man whom I had discipled.

Before the church service began, I saw the lawyer and his sons. I was so excited! I thought, "This woman is at least allowing her sons to come to church again." God had worked so fast. I couldn't expect Him to do much more. The man came over and introduced me to his sons. Then he said, "I want you to meet someone else."

I turned around to see this tall, beautiful, glowing woman. He said, "This is my wife." I was absolutely ecstatic! She said, "He talks about you all the time. You really helped him." She went on to say, "I wrote a letter to my dad. I haven't mailed it, but I have forgiven him."

God had changed what I thought was a hopeless situation in basically no time. But it didn't end there. The lawyer's wife continued, "My husband and I talked and I explained to him that he was doing some things which hurt our relationship." Her husband went into the situation thinking that his wife needed to change, not realizing that he did too!

With God's amazing grace, He had changed the man and his wife.

We can't change our spouses, but God can change us if we yield to Him. Consider 1 Peter 3:1, 2: "Wives, in the same way be submissive to your husbands so that, if any of them do not believe the word (God's Word), they may be won over without words by the behavior of their wives, when they see the purity and reverence of your lives." The biblical principle here is that *a changed behavior speaks louder than words* to those with which we have a close relationship.

Men, if these wives can change for the better, then we men can too! We have the same empowering Holy Spirit living in us!

Let Philippians 1:6 be an encouragement to you. It says, "Being confident of this, that He who began a good work in you will carry it on to completion until the day of Christ Jesus."

Re-Opening a Closed Spirit

I think it is safe to say that more than a few of us intentionally or unintentionally have closed the spirit of our spouse at one time or another in our marriage.

If this is true, then how do we reopen the spirit of our beloved spouse?

There are a few steps you need to take in order to re-open a closed spirit:

•Become _soft_ and _tender_ with the person. Proverbs 15:1: "A gentle answer turns away wrath, but a hard word stirs up anger." Basically, it takes two to fight. No matter what the other person is saying to you, don't become defensive. You are attempting to help your spouse who is wounded.

•_Understand_, as much as possible, what the other person is going through.

•Remember, listen to what is being said, do not react to the words used. Try to _hear the essence_ of what was said. You may not understand your spouse's pain but do the best you can in trying. Sometimes, even when we are trying to help our spouse, she may say hurtful words because we may be the only ones to which she can truly express her feelings. This too is part of the intimacy. We also need to understand that we are trying to help her right now. Later, when we are healthy, we may be able to help our spouse to communicate with us in a more effective way. Sometimes, we hear one particular word and/or phrase and we don't hear anything else. We just begin formulating our "comeback." In the late 60's, I attended an all black high school. Our English teacher had a white speaker address our class. During his talk, he used the word _nigger_. As soon as he left, we asked our teacher why she had him speak to us. We told her what she had already heard, "He used the 'N' word." She asked, "Did you hear what else he said?" We said, "No." She went on to tell us that he said, "People shouldn't use the word *nigger* because it has a derogatory connotation." We were shocked and pleased. We asked, "What else did he say?" She told us, "You should have been listening." Sometimes, we have words which serve as "hot buttons." Once we hear them, we won't hear anything else. We need to eliminate these "hot buttons" from our vocabulary if we are to hear and understand our spouses, especially when they are wounded, and especially if we have caused the wound.

•*Recognize* that the other person is hurting and *acknowledge any wrong* you may have done in provoking their anger. If you have caused the pain, then apologize. Don't say, "If I have hurt you, please forgive me." This isn't an apology. If you have caused the pain, regardless of it being intentional or unintentional, accept the responsibility. Be a man. Say to her, "Honey, I'm so sorry I hurt you. Will you please forgive me?" If it was unintentional, then say, "Honey (use your own nickname for her), I'm so sorry I hurt you. I didn't mean to, but I now realize I hurt you and will you please forgive me?"

James 1:20: "For man's anger does not bring a righteous life that God desires."

Ephesians 4:26: "In your anger, do not sin."

Anger is not a sin, but it can lead to sin.

•If possible, *touch* the other person *gently* in a *non-sexual* way (sometimes they need space). If she says, "Don't touch me!" I strongly suggest you don't touch her. Touching in a non-sexual way can be therapeutic. So if she lets you touch her, then hold her hand or hug her. The average woman likes to be hugged 8 to 10 times a day in a non-sexual way. Don't do what a guy at one of our marriage conferences did. He got my attention and said, "I'm going to start that right now." He started bouncing his wife off his chest rapidly, counting, "One, two, three, …." If you are going to implement this practice, take your time and hug your wife—and don't count or mark how many times on your mirror or refrigerator.

•Seek _forgiveness_ and _wait_ for a _response_. Biblically, the _stronger_ person always _initiates_ the _peace_. When I say to wait for a response, sometimes our spouses can't forgive us right away. We are built differently emotionally. Some women, certainly not all, need more time to process some issues because they are holistic (this can be true of some men, so know your spouse). If your wife should say to you, "I can't forgive you right now," then you need to ask her, "When can you forgive me?" The purpose is from the biblical principle in 1 Corinthians 7:5 about coming back together. The text here is about sex, but I'd like to make an application about being one—not sex, but intimacy (ask your wife if you don't understand this). Also, Ephesians 4:26 speaks of us, "Not letting the sun go down on our wrath—anger." The longer we let tension go unresolved, the more we play into Satan's hand. In Revelation 12:10b, Satan is called the accuser. Satan will come to you and your spouse and cause you to accuse each other falsely. For example, he'll say to me, "Clarence, Brenda knows better than that, she is trying to be the head without saying." Or he will go to Brenda and say, "How long are going to keep telling that Negro that and he still ain't listening. He's trying to force you to submit. You'd better be careful, girl!" We have to be careful not to fall for this trip. A speedy time of forgiveness makes this scenario less likely to happen or to have much impact on the relationship. So Brenda and I encourage couples not to go more than two days without resolving their conflict. This does three things: (1) It allows the more emotional and/or holistic spouse to process their pain and still be who they are; (2) This practice doesn't allow a spouse to remain upset indefinitely and/or have a "pity" party, giving an open door to Satan to cause division; and (3) Hopefully, the spouse who is upset will ask himself/herself, "Why does what he/she said and/or did upset me so much?" Such a question, may lead to an answer, resulting in their spiritual growth.

•To wives: (1 Peter 3:1) Win men/husbands with _action_. Don't nag or preach.

•To husbands: (1 Peter 3:7) God will _not_ hear the prayers of one not _treating_ his wife _properly_. Don't be one way at church and another at home. Such inconsistent actions handicap your children as well as your spouse. It makes it difficult for them to trust you. There's no place in marriage for physical or mental abuse.

•Never, Never, Give Up!

These bullet points came from _FamilyLife's A Weekend to Remember_ manual. I explained them to you here as I often do in seminar presentations.

How's Your Prayer Life?

Sometimes our difficulties in life drive us to pray. I love Philippians 4:6, 7: "Do not be anxious for anything, but in everything, by prayer and petitions, with thanksgiving, present your requests to God. And the peace of God, which transcends all understanding, will guard your hearts and minds in Christ Jesus."

I love these verses because they tell me that nothing is too small or big for me to take to God. I'm not bothering Him. He wants to spend time with me (Psalm 5:3; 1 Corinthians 1:9). God just warns me to pray with the right motives (James

4:3). James 5:16-18 states, "Therefore, confess your sins to each other and pray for each other so that you may be healed. The prayer of a righteous man is *powerful* and *effective* (Christ has made us righteous). Elijah was a *man just like us.* He prayed earnestly that it would not rain, and it did not rain on the land for three and a half years. Again he prayed, and the heavens gave rain, and the earth produced its crops."

We're not asking God to stop the rain, we just want our wives to let us watch ESPN or the "big game" without interruption. This would be a miracle!!

Who Are You Talking To?

As mentioned earlier in this book, I think most men need someone with whom they can talk and trust. If you are in a difficult marriage, it is good therapy for you to have a Christian brother to talk to, ask questions, and pray with you for your wife, children (if you have any) and you. You don't need any army, because some of the things you share you don't want getting back to your wife. She may not understand your emotions or the context of your conversation about your marriage.

If you don't have a Christian brother like this, then ask God for one. Don't wait until you are in a crisis. It is difficult to prepare for the crisis during the crisis!

Practice Can Make A Difference (The Reciprocity Principle)

Have you ever received a Christmas gift from someone with whom you weren't close? Instead of being excited about the gift, it was somewhat depressing because you immediately felt obligated to get this person a gift next Christmas. Is anybody feeling me?

Well, the reciprocity principle works this way. Look at it from a positive perspective. If we do, we have rediscovered the *Golden Rule*.

A Moody Bible Institute chapel changed my life. I don't remember the speaker, but he mentioned putting the Golden Rule into action. In fact, he called it *afterglow*. He said as a preacher, he would often get excited about spiritual growth and promise his wife he would do better. It usually lasted three weeks. He said he stopped telling his wife what he was going to do and just did it. It revolutionized his marriage!

I thought I'd try it at home with my Mom. I loved my Mom (she's in heaven now), but we often had a hard time getting along in the same house for an extended period of time, especially when I had returned from playing basketball overseas. She would say to me, "I don't care where you have been, who you have become, but as long as you are staying under my roof, you are going to obey my rules." She was killing me.

But I remembered the chapel message. I began to do things the first time she asked and sometimes before she asked (I didn't do things before she asked all the time—I didn't want to give her a heart attack). As my Mom saw me change, to my amazement, she did too!

Men, practice the principles in this chapter. They will change you, your spouse, and your marriage.

How to Find a Helpful Christian Counselor

Some marriage situations require more than the couple can do themselves. Some couples may need the assistance of a pastor and/or a professional Christian counselor.

Unfortunately, as a pastor, I've seen some counselors Christian and non-Christian do more damage than good. I have only a few to whom I refer people. I have asked Christopher McCluskey, a trained and certified Christian sex therapist and life coach, how to find an effective Christian counselor. He is no longer receiving clients, but he has some tremendous insights people need to consider when seeking a counselor or therapist:

"Interview potential therapists before deciding to hire them. The quality of their personhood is of such greater importance than perhaps any other type of professional with whom you might contract, because they will be helping to shape the way you move through one of the most difficult seasons of your life, and the lessons you learn as a result of it. Psychotherapy has probably done more damage on a one-on-one basis than any other profession, as they've encouraged people to 'look out for number one,' get a divorce and move on, re-evaluate your moral foundations, etc.

"Some therapists will talk with you by phone for an inquiry at no charge. Ask about their clinical training and licensure, and any certifications in specific areas of specialization. Also ask how long they've been in practice and if they can provide a reference or two. Endorsements from local pastors whom you respect are really valuable—pastors refer to therapists all the time and they usually have a **very** short list of those they trust. Naturally, you'll want to know how they integrate their Christianity into their practice. I wouldn't consider going to a therapist who isn't a Christian—that's all there is to it. However, the simple fact that they say they're Christian doesn't tell you much. You need to ask how they integrate their faith. Will they pray with you? Do they know the

Word and apply it as their guide for practice? Do they ask the Holy Spirit to minister through them? These are just suggestions for some questions to ask.

"You can usually tell pretty quickly if it's going to be a 'fit' or not. Try to get recommendations from trusted friends and your pastor before you even start calling therapists—don't start with the Yellow Pages. It's just too critical of a decision."

I hope you find Christopher's suggestions helpful.

Cheaper to Keep Her

If you are in a difficult marriage, then you have probably thought (or are thinking right now) about divorcing your wife. Don't beat yourself up with guilty feelings about having this thought. It's only natural to want to get out of what appears to be a bad situation as soon as possible. But look at the bigger picture and don't forget the God factor.

Let me suggest to you that it is cheaper to keep her. I'm not making light of divorce. But I am trying to make you think. Think of the emotional scarring that your friends who have divorced are still carrying. Think about the emotional pain of children you have known who have seen their parents divorce. Have you heard their thoughts about marriage since their parents' divorce? Ask a child whose parents divorced about their new views regarding marriage. Think of the emotional stress with your church and work resulting from your divorce. I'm not even mentioning lawyer fees, court costs, and alimony.

It is much cheaper and healthier to work through a difficult marriage in order to reach a new level of intimacy, than to divorce and start all over again with the baggage of a previous divorce.

There is no time limit and it's not too late. One woman during one of my teaching sessions told me that for 32 years, her husband had a drinking problem. He wasn't a Christian. All her friends told her to leave him. Instead, she kept praying and one day, he asked Christ to come into his life. Christ did, he stopped drinking and he led all three of his adult children to Christ. Now all of his grandchildren are Christians and they all go to church together.

This isn't about judging anyone. I'm just sharing the experience of two decades of marriage, conducting marriage seminars, and pre-marital and marriage counseling.

May God bless you as you work through your marriage difficulties. It has tremendous potential for incredible intimacy and oneness if you are willing to work through difficulty and don't quit.

Working through your difficult marriage is worth it!

Action Points
Chapter Six
When All Hell Breaks Loose

1. When you encounter difficulty in your marriage, is your first step to blame your wife? Why or why not?

2. Do you examine the situation to see if you are at fault? Which step, if any, is this for you?

3. Do you have a male friend with whom you can discuss your marriage and will he keep it confidential?

4. Does this same friend if you have one, care enough about you and your wife to tell you what you may not want to hear, but need to hear or is he just your cheerleader?

5. Do you think your wife or you need counseling? If yes, will the two of you go together? (Dr. McCluskey's suggestions for finding a Christian counselor may prove invaluable.)

6. Since divorce is not the best solution to marital difficulty, what is going to be your first step towards resolving the problem(s) in your marriage? Consider asking your wife to join you in counseling because you want help (you do want help for your marriage don't you?). This is a way of getting both of you in counseling without blaming your wife.

7. Remember that your marriage didn't get in this situation overnight and probably won't be resolved overnight. What will you do to help you remain patient?

8. Write a prayer, asking God for His help in your marriage and the strength not to give up on it. Don't quit. You are not alone!

Chapter Seven
A Vow To Cherish:
When Your Wife
Can No Longer Be Your Best Friend

Harrison Ford, one of my favorite actors, departed from his usual action movie roles to star in *Regarding Henry*. As the film begins, Henry is a big city "power attorney" who just won a major case—translating into a huge sum of money for his firm. Henry's victory was unethical, but he didn't get caught so he didn't care.

Returning home from his firm's celebration party, Henry stopped by a convenience store for cigarettes. While there, the store was robbed, and in the chaos Henry was shot in the head. As a result, this power attorney loses his memory of almost everything, including how to walk. He becomes an adult child, having to grow up again. One day his longtime housekeeper said, "I like this Mr. Henry." Physically, he was much the same; maybe a bit slower moving. Emotionally and mentally, however, Henry was a different person.

Some of us go to movies for a brief escape from real life. But what do we do when we are living real life with someone who has become a different person? What do we do when our situation doesn't end after two or three hours, but instead is everyday life?

We often hear that movies simply imitate real life. For some men, *Regarding Henry* is real life, except we might change the title to *Regarding Helen*.

This chapter is for men whose wives are still alive, but have a mental and/or physical illness and are unable to continue being the best friend of their husbands. They have become like Henry. Some of these ladies no longer even recognize these special men as their husbands.

Initially, I intended to interview such husbands. But after interviewing the first husband, I decided his life experience will encourage all hearts who read this chapter.

I've asked my new friend to share his story of his life as caregiver for his wife, who is now mentally unable to be his best friend. This chapter isn't a solution, but hopefully, will be an encouragement that

- •You are not the only man wrestling with this situation,
- •Some of the wildest thoughts you may have had about God and your spouse aren't crazy or abnormal (I'm not saying they are right, but understandable in your present circumstances),
- •You will see how some men in situations much like yours are functioning, and maybe most important,
- •You'll know that someone cares for you. Life is still worth living.

One Man's Story

My interviewee will remain anonymous out of respect for his family's privacy. He and his wife have been married since 1981. It is his first marriage, her second. Her condition began eleven years into their marriage and may have been triggered by issues affecting the children from her first marriage. Here is his story, primarily in his own words:

"It seemed to begin when our daughter started having some difficulties. She was missing pieces of her childhood. She could never be assertive. That was unusual for a child. Then we would see her in the choir with a different demeanor, like a different person, singing in front of the whole group.

"She was a very caring, very special girl. But then we began to hear two voices as she came up the driveway after school. When we looked to see who our daughter had brought home, she was the only one in sight. Also, there were pieces of time that she couldn't recall.

"We got her into counseling and went through five years of hell. We found out that the two oldest children were sexually abused not by their father, but by people he set up to spend time with the children. Our daughter had split off multiple—double figures in number—personalities to protect herself as a little girl. (Amazingly, today she is doing well. With the help of a Christian counselor, a wonderful lady, she came out of her situation.)

"All of a sudden, my wife began to have flashbacks about the physical abuse and sexual rape her first husband put her through. She was a mess. She began to unravel. We finally got her on some medication. Still, there were days when she would wrap herself up in a ball and not be functional.

"My wife became jealous of the time I spent with male friends. She thought that we should be able to have that kind of time together, that we were enough for each other. I was clearly not satisfied with the prospect of no time with friends outside of my marriage. I had my issues with the dysfunction in our relationship.

"I was working fulltime, and work became difficult. In the middle of all this, I had to release three staff. Their attacks became part of the work climate. But as difficult as work was, it was a respite for me. It was a break from being at home.

"I would pray constantly. Having family support was invaluable. I leaned on my family a lot. I cried on the phone a lot. I had male friends to whom I could vent (and they would let me) and talk over my situation. I could ask for prayer. They would also offer suggestions.

"What happened internally and emotionally was pretty rough because the woman I married was no longer the woman I had. I had no physical relationship with her. It is a difficult thing because you have so much emotional hurt, it's hard to get close. She wanted to get close, but with no emotional connection. In a way, our roles switched. I was the one longing for real affection as we made love, and my wife seemed to have cared less. And I told her, 'I can't. I feel like I'm prostituting myself. We have got to have a relationship.'

"It was through this that I asked God, 'What is this? What is going on?' You have to go through the struggles, even when they don't make sense.

"As a young man, I prayed for my future wife before I knew her. I'm talking about all through my teen years, that she would be holy, that she would be chaste. I prayed that He would protect her, mold her and make her an able, capable helpmate. I married a divorced woman with three children (we had two more through our union). With eyes wide open, I entered this situation. She did not purposely deceive me.

"As we walked through our trauma together, her last counselor reminded me of the long haul this will be. On our way out the door, the counselor said, 'I'm going to be working with your wife a lot here.'

"Our marriage counselor also gave me some good insight, even though it was hard to hear. She said, 'You know that she will never be the same. And likely after the therapy, you'll be married to a different woman. Because what you married isn't who she is!'

"How do you deal with that? Sure people change over the years, but not the whole essence of who they are. It's just that my wife was so wounded that she could never flower in her first marriage. She was traumatized and never developed. So now, there is this *other* woman coming out.

"Added to that, the medication becomes a difficulty because I began wondering over the years, and even more so this past year, how much of her problem is medication-related and how much is mental health-related? She went through psychological tests and she was all over the place. It was a mix; she didn't fit one clear diagnosis.

"But this was a wonderful woman I married. She treated me well. I married my best friend. I never had a friend as close as she. This 'best friend' status has been hard to hold onto. Frankly, I'm not ready to say that I'm there right now. I'm a friend of hers, but even that wasn't always the case.

"My wife had a lot of demands on me during her most difficult days because of the need and the hurt. Some of it, I just couldn't do. For example, I couldn't hold her all evening. It is impractical when you have five kids. Our five children, who ranged in age from high school to pre-school, needed attention. I had to cover food, laundry, housecleaning, errands, one-on-one time and love, homework, preparation for school the next day, and getting them to bed.

"Each child had their own dynamics, with their own questions: 'What's happening to this family? Is this blowing apart? Are we going to be a family? What happened to my mom?' Each of the kids had enough memory to know that she changed. So there was the whole dynamic of them having to cope with the loss of their mother and having a different mother now. Even today, I still have to help them cope while I'm trying to cope.

"There was a time when I had to go in for counseling because I needed someone with whom to talk to help me sort out some of this stuff. The situation was just too severe. There was a time when our entire family had therapy weekly. The insurance was paying for it, but I had to make the copays. You can't imagine the expense, but I had no choice if I was to keep my family together.

"There are some good secular counselors out there, but Christian counselors are better because they meet you with your, let me say it in a secular way, 'with your belief system.' That's what they work from.

"But the deliberation of faith in this is saying, 'Okay, I have to come to grips. Is God's Word accurate? What is the role of sin and fallenness in the world? What can I own and what can I not?' That's the issue. 'What crutch am I using during all this pain and is that beneficial? What am I doing in relation to church, spiritual feeding, and discipleship for myself?'

Question: How did you feel about God in regards to losing the wife you married and gaining a new wife?

"There were so many unknown, unexpected things happening. I felt loss of control in managing the household. In a sense, my family was escaping me and I asked that proverbial question: 'God, why? I never lifted a hand to her. I'm not a violent man. I didn't swear at her. All of this is inappropriate for a man to do.'

"Then I had to remind myself that God's Word is true. I had to do the gut-check: Is He true in the valley as well as the hilltop, even when I don't feel it? I don't think I had a crisis of faith, but I needed a lot of reassurance that God was there.

"Is God there? I can't imagine not believing. But if He isn't there in times like this, what else is there? But for me, it's trying to put the pieces together enough so you can make some sense of it. So part my deliberation was to make some sense of all these thoughts running through my head and put them to some use. Scripture speaks about the 'God of all comfort,' and that we can comfort others when we have experienced comfort (2 Corinthians 1:3-5).

"I sought to do some study; I would talk through and mentally process biblical truths. For example, 'All things work together for good for those who are called according to His purpose.' (Romans 8:28) That doesn't mean all things are good, but it means that God can rise above any kind of fallen circumstance and bring good from it. So what is that *good*? A part is compassion, a part is empathy, which in my own work setting is quite amazing to define.

"I now have a better of understanding of domestic violence and its impact on women, children and the next marriage.

"I looked at biblical characters. What do you think Hosea went through? He married a woman. He was chaste, a prophet of God. What did she do with him? She went back to streetwalking. And what did God tell Hosea to do? God told Hosea, 'Go back and get her, I have a lesson to teach you. You're a *living life* lesson for Israel as a prophet. You think that you are going to have it easy as a prophet—I (God) just give you some words and you tell the people? Guess what, you get to live it!'

"So that's another piece is when you are rooted in the Word. Fortunately, I had a lot of rooting. If you have a lot to draw from, Scripture verses just flow in your mind. In reading God's Word, you see things in a new light because you are hashing it over. You're comparing Scripture with Scripture and you start coming up with these things.

"It is not for me to know why. It is for me to be obedient; because who is it that I love? Who is it that loved me first?"

"I was a despicable sinner who did not deserve anything from the Lord, only His wrath. But He gave me grace and adopted me into His household. I wasn't perfect, so why am I expecting perfection in my life?

"So there are pieces like that. But it doesn't mean that I haven't struggled with thinking, 'I need to divorce her. No, I can't divorce her. What are the biblical grounds? Is she a bad woman or a good woman? She really is a good woman, even through all of this. She is not mean-spirited, she's not vindictive. She's not immoral.' And so there are those pieces that I had to work through.

"She can function for a while and then, she has to shut down. She does have daily cycles where she has to take naps in the morning and the afternoon.

"One Mental Health Board of Directors believes 90% of marriages end in divorce when one spouse has a chronic mental health condition. Most spouses would have found greener pastures elsewhere instead of going through this valley and still, to some extent, living in the desert of unfulfillment. A lot of wounding takes place, a lot of challenges to one's tidy theological constructs, but from the trials and tribulations so personal and close to home, there is much to be gained. You learn more about yourself going through the hard times than you ever could if things sailed along more smoothly. It has sensitized my heart and expanded my compassion in very many ways. As the wounding and sorrow took place over many years, so the healing is also taking time.

"The Christian community just doesn't talk about this topic, yet one in four of five women will suffer with some kind of mental health problem during their lifetime. Most will have husbands. What I have heard from the community of faith tends to be trite and uninformed answers to these difficult situations.

*Question: What advice would you give
to men experiencing similar circumstances?*

My new friend shared with me the following list in
response to my question:

1. When you are in pain, all you see is the pain. Step back
because the pain isn't forever!
2. You have to be hard and soft. You can't take the easy
way out because of what it does to you and others.
3. Talk to God about everything daily.
4. Look for good times you can have even during imper-
fect circumstances.
5. Be aware that you will want to connect emotionally
and often your spouse can't.
6. You will need nurturing because you will often feel the
life is sucked out of you (find someone who is healthy).
7. You will have to make adjustments: sexually, at work,
in your family.
8. For support, ask for help outside of family, lose
friends who can't understand.
9. Rediscover God's grace: "I don't have to be perfect,
even in the midst of my hurt." (But don't make this a
license to sin).
10. God won't forsake you. He will be your **best** friend.
11. Why not divorce?
   a. God hates divorce.
   b. Remember the wedding vow: "For better or for
   worse."
   c. Ask, "What is the loving thing to do for spouse and
   children?"
   d. With divorce, children worry about losing their
   father after they have already lost their mother
   (mentally and/or emotionally).

e. If you are considering divorce, do you have a biblical basis?

12. Is my vow worth the pain?

13. The issue is integrity—will I keep working on it?

14. Look beyond the moment of the pain and look from the perspective of a lifetime.

15. The situation has created in me a passion for other people's pain because they are ever-living souls.

16. Romans 8:28: "And we know that in all things God works for the good of those who love Him, who have been called according to His purpose." As a Christian, do I really believe this? Is it true? Am I living like it is true? Look for practical ways God is making it true for you.

17. Remember that God has been with you in the past. This will help you to trust Him for the present and the future. Remember the goodness of God.

"When you are going through the pain, all you feel is the emotional pain. You are absorbed by the moment or the circumstance. You don't necessarily see any hope, but at some point, you have to step back out of that. You have to realize that what you are experiencing or the way you feel won't last forever.

"In order to go through a valley, you have to go over a hill. Life isn't all a valley. So you need to realize that the ache and the pain you feel now won't last.

"Somewhere in the Bible, part of a verse says, '…and it shall come to pass.' I grabbed a hold of that idea and said to myself, 'This too will pass, and just because you are going through it doesn't mean it won't pass. The way you feel now may not be what you feel tomorrow, the next week, the next month, the next year.'

"My wife still has her issues. She has her good days and bad ones. She is on medication, which she is taking for the next month. Her good days are getting better. And I'm discovering that I'm healing, I'm actually healing. I'm able to reach out to people much more. I'm more empathic, I listen, I can understand.

"In fact, I was at Wal-Mart a couple nights ago, and I looked at all those faces of people, realizing that these are *never-dying, ever-living souls.* Every soul of each person never dies. They are either heading one direction or the other. And they have their own life experiences."

Be Encouraged

Quite an experience, isn't it? Our brother is still living through the trauma of a spouse who cannot be the same, but it seems that he is on the other side now, past the initial shock and now learning lifelong lessons from this particular life experience. We can all learn from a man, a real man who didn't run away from his responsibility, but demonstrated to his wife, children, his family, the medical profession, and to himself what it means to live out your faith when life doesn't seem fair.

It's not over for him. As I interviewed him he shared that his best friend, the guy with whom he could talk about everything, moved out of town. Somehow, I think he will survive this loss too!

My new friend isn't Superman. He simply has leaned and continues to lean on a Super God! This same God is available to you at any time. If you don't know Him, just ask Him to forgive you for your sins and to come into your life. He can live through and empower in the Person of the Holy Spirit. You, too can make it through this trial and remember, it won't last forever!

Action Points
Chapter Seven
When Your Wife Can No Longer Be Your Best Friend

1. Review my friend's suggestions to men who have similar circumstances. What three suggestions can you put into practice this week?

2. What about my friend's story encourages you not to quit?

3. Do you have a support group: family, church, people outside of family? If not, who will you contact this week to become a source of support for you?

4. How might it help you to "take one day at a time" with your spouse?

5. What will you do to take time for yourself to get refreshed? Write three ideas here, and put one into practice in the next two days.

6. Seek to discover what lessons God may be teaching you. What lessons have you already learned that you can pass on to others?

7. What can you learn from the story in this chapter to help you deal with your initial responses to—and even depression about—a "special needs" spouse?

8. Do you have one male friend with whom you can talk about anything at any time? If so, great! If not, write a few possibilities here.

9. What can you do to maintain appropriate friendships with women, especially if your wife and you can no longer be sexually intimate?

10. What can you do this week to create or enhance a "safe place" for your children (if you have children)? How will you give them hope with your physical touch, words, and example of living life?

11. If you aren't a Christian, then the last page of this chapter will help you to become one. Simply ask Jesus Christ to forgive you for your sins and come into your life. Ask Him to now lead your life, then "Thank" Jesus Christ for coming into your life. These words aren't magic, but if you are sincere, Christ will come into your life. He may or may not change the circumstances, but He will certainly change you. This is the best life experience you can possibly have!

Chapter Eight
Kiss of Death: The Secret Sin of Pornography

The goal of every married man is to keep his wife as his best friend. Every mutually beneficial marriage requires constant work. No husband needs—or wants—any additional burden working against his marriage.

Pornography, one of the fastest growing vices in our culture, constantly weighs in against healthy marriages. It's a burden we don't need. Each day, pornography causes more husbands to lose their wives as their best friends.

Let's be clear: I know pornography isn't just a "male thing." Women also struggle with pornography. But I'm focusing on husbands or husbands-to-be in this chapter.

At the marriage conferences Brenda and I have conducted within the last year, I've felt led to publicly discuss my eleven-year addiction to, and deliverance from, pornography. Brenda has graciously allowed me to do this because, somehow, my public confession of this hideous secret sin helps couples at the conferences. In fact, some couples have shared with me that my discussing it publicly has saved their marriages.

With every hope that God will use this to help your marriage, here's my story.

The Seduction of Pornography: My Own Story

How do we get seduced into pornography? A coffee buddy of mine laid it out like this: "The pornography imprinted on the pages become imprinted on the mind." In other words, *what you see becomes what you think.* Pornography creates visual temptation and mental sexual sin. Is it any wonder it causes problems for more than a few of us husbands who want to keep our wives as our best friends?

I don't enjoy detailing my fall into pornography, but I do enjoy telling others about God's gracious deliverance. I honestly believe that sharing my personal battle will help some of you to know that I've been where you are. What I'm about to say is real, not some made-up story to which no one can relate.

And here's the good news: God has delivered me in spite of myself. He can and will deliver you, if you ask Him.

Pornography addicts can be single or married, of any color, creed, or economic background. We're athletes, we're computer programmers, we're pastors, we're custodians, we're truck drivers, we're CEOs. What binds us together is an addiction to visual images that imprint our minds and lead to mental—and perhaps physical—sexual sin.

Sadly enough, many men are introduced to pornography before the age of ten. These men usually found their father's stash of pornography magazines.

Some single men believe they use pornography to keep themselves pure. Their thinking is that they're safe if they simply masturbate to a seductive picture instead of "going all the way" on a date. But sexual purity is a matter of the mind and heart, according to Jesus. Consider his perspective as found in Matthew 5:19: "But I tell you that anyone who *looks* at a woman lustfully has already committed adultery with her in his heart." How can you stop looking at women lustfully? Consider them your sister created in God's image. Period.

The same goes for married men, of course.

My prayer for any of you struggling with pornography is that this chapter will help you find freedom from this addiction. Again, I want to remind you that there is hope for you. My personal struggle was even more difficult because during my eleven-year addiction, I felt there was no one I could talk to about it.

I was wrong. I had friends and I needed to trust them. No one can break the addiction of pornography for you but God and someone to whom you can be accountable. (A biblical, Christian counselor certainly can help.) I now have someone to whom I can be accountable. It's made a remarkable difference for me.

Why is someone else's perspective so important in dealing with pornography addiction? Well, I certainly never saw it coming. If someone would have told me that I—a guy who had been preaching the Gospel of Jesus Christ for twelve years—would become addicted to pornography, I wouldn't have believed it myself! How could it happen?

Frankly, I was ripe for it. I was a 29-year-old virgin, and my sex drive was killing me. I was new to town. Single Christian girls with whom I could even talk were nowhere to be found. For me, having girls around to talk to as friends has always helped me to see them as people. When they weren't around, it was easy for me to view them as simply sex objects. So, regretfully, I did. Are you old enough to remember the song, *I'm A Girl Watcher*? I was definitely a "girl-watcher." It wasn't easy to change this first-step habit toward pornography. First, you admire women with their clothes on. The natural progression is to want to see them without their clothes.

Jesus often had women who were His friends around Him. I always wondered if that helped Him keep His sex drive under control? He was fully human and fully God. As a man He probably had a sex drive, even if He never acted on it. Hebrews 4:15 says, "For we do not have a high priest who is unable to sympathize with our weaknesses, but we have one who has been tempted in **every** way, *just as we are*—yet without sin."

I believe Jesus understands our struggle in this area. *And it may be a good practice to develop friendships with single women for the sole purpose of being "just friends."*

I was a fulltime Christian worker in a supposedly Christian environment. That should have created a buffer zone or safe place for me, but it was just the opposite. Former Colorado University football coach and President of Promise Keepers, Bill McCartney, at the 1996 Atlanta Pastors' Conference said that, "Seventy percent of men in ministry have had an affair or inappropriate conduct with women." A lot of them must have been from the city where I was working. You see, my job was working with pastors. More than a few of them in this particular city had a reputation for womanizing.

My required membership was in an historic and prestigious church, which didn't have any single Christian girls my age. Maybe the preaching of religion for religion's sake, self-effort, and the impracticality of the religion being preached wasn't appealing to my peers—neither was the life-changing Jesus Christ, nor the indwelling Holy Spirit empowering us to live a daily, victorious life, preached from the pulpit.

My pastor—who was also my boss—daily bragged to me of his reputation of being sexually active until he got too old to continue. Sleeping around was encouraged, even by the pastors. Some of the men in church thought that I was a homosexual because I wasn't "sleeping around" and I didn't have a girlfriend. My pastor's chauffeur told me, "You should be humping (having sex) every night."

It would be easy to blame my addiction on my environment or my circumstances, but I am totally responsible for the wrong choices I made. No one held a gun to my head. I refused to listen to the voice of the Holy Spirit *yelling* at me not to watch pornography. It would have been helpful to have had godly men to set an example for me. I didn't, but it is still no excuse.

Did I mention that more than one married woman at this prestigious church had propositioned me? One pastor in town suggested that I date his secretary. I later discovered that he was hoping that we would date, so if she became pregnant, it would be assumed that the baby was mine. Supposedly this pastor was sleeping with his secretary, even though he was married with eight children at the time. His present wife had been the former babysitter for him and his first wife.

This was quite a town for adultery and divorce among pastors. In fact, one out-of-town pastor who came to preach was told by my pastor in my presence, "I'll get your alcohol, but you've got to get your own women." These men often traveled to conventions, flying their wives *and* mistresses in to join them. The police and newspapers said that when these conventions of this particular denomination were held in their cities, alcohol sales and prostitution went up!

I was Director of Christian Education for the eastern half of the state. When I was asked to teach a seminar, I always insisted on teaching evangelism because it seemed that so many of these *Christian* state leaders didn't have a personal relationship with Jesus Christ, or at least didn't live like it. Even though I wasn't married, I taught biblical marriage principles as often as possible because of the sexual immorality present in the Christian circles I frequented.

How did it happen? I was lonely. I had no Christian fellowship from my peers and no accountability partner. I seemed surrounded by people with no regard for sexual purity. I had no women friends my age I could treat as sisters in Christ.

These are not excuses. Instead, maybe they're warning signs I should have recognized.

It happened one night, while I was staying at the home of my boss and pastor. He and his wife had gone to bed. I stayed up to watch TV. I didn't have a TV at my apartment, so this was a treat for me. I was flipping channels searching for something to watch to unwind. I hit the *Playboy* channel—and left it there. The women were undressing and having sex everywhere!

My eyes were pleased, yet I felt guilty immediately. I knew that I shouldn't be watching this stuff. But instead of turning the TV off, I turned the volume down. I tried to listen to hear if my hosts were coming down the hall. I kept my finger strategically positioned on the TV remote, so I could change the channel at a moment's notice and appear innocent.

Can anybody relate to this? I couldn't believe my eyes, nor could I see enough. I thought, "I know this is wrong, but this is *only one night*. I'm never going to do this again, and I'm not committing a sin with someone else. I know it is wrong, but God will forgive me." Whether it was Satan's lie to me or me lying to myself, I bought it. Satan didn't tell me about the long-term addiction, the guilt, the secrecy, the fear of being discovered—only to *enjoy the moment!*

I was up into the wee hours of the next morning. In bed that night, I fantasized about having sex with the women. I masturbated in the bed and loved it. The release and sensation felt so *good!* I was hooked! I was a virgin. I knew I wasn't going to have sex with anyone before I got married. So what was the harm in getting a release? I wasn't hurting anyone. My self-deception gave me no idea of what I was *willingly* getting myself into.

I was ashamed. I felt so guilty. I knew that I needed to ask God to forgive me, but I somehow wanted to earn the right to come before Him. This is another of Satan's lies. I bought into the "You're a preacher, so your sin is greater. How can God forgive you?" routine. But I couldn't do anything to be right on my own before God, and neither can you. My helplessness was overwhelming and depressing.

The only thing I could do to get right with God was ask, accept and believe in God's unconditional forgiveness. There were still consequences for my sin, but God totally forgives. Psalms 103:10, 12 describe God's forgiveness: "He does not treat us as our sins deserve or repay us according to our iniquities....As far as the east is from the west, so far has He removed our transgressions from us." It is a gift. You have to come as you are and accept Christ's forgiveness. God makes us righteous.

So there I was, signed, sealed, delivered, and forgiven. My problems with pornography were over, right? Hardly. My thoughts gravitated to pornography when my mind wasn't occupied with other plans or responsibilities. I didn't have a TV, but bought a few *Playboy* magazines, even masturbating once in awhile while looking at one of these magazines.

Up and down stretches of self-denial were common. I kept telling myself, "I can stop whenever I want to." Sound familiar? I was up and down spiritually too. The cycle was sinning, confessing the sin, asking for forgiveness—promising never to do it again, never wanting to do it again, feeling good and clean again, but somehow finding myself watching pornography again and again. I was supposed to be one of the more spiritual men in town. In truth, I was no better than the worst of the pastors committing adultery. It was just that in my case, no one knew but me about my **secret sin.**

One Saturday night in the spring of 1984, I watched pornography which led to masturbating. The next morning, I was to preach in one of my favorite churches in the state. I loved this church and its godly pastor. I drove two hours one way each week to teach discipleship, my passion (yeah, I know it sounds crazy to be addicted to pornography and loving discipleship—*there's no logic to sin*), to this church's leadership. I would stay over that night, usually at the senior pastor's home, and drive back the next morning.

I struggled with not confessing my sin and trying to preach as though everything was right in my relationship with God. I debated with God during the two-hour drive to this church. Before I got up to preach, the pastor introduced me as this "godly, pure, young man amidst many immoral preachers." He prayed that I would stay pure.

As I stood to begin preaching, I was so convicted by the Holy Spirit that I confessed my sin (but not with specifics from the night before); then, the tears came. I finally gained my composure and preached my sermon.

The response to the sermon was the most unusual that I had seen up to that point in my life. No one moved. Usually, at least kids made frequent bathroom runs, but this day, no one did. I gave the invitation to this sermon on *forgiveness*, challenging parents to forgive their children and for children to forgive their parents. It seemed like revival broke out! The people actually began right there in church asking each other for forgiveness. I sensed the power of God as never before. It seemed that during my brief time of brokenness and humility, God used me as His vessel to communicate His incredible love. I was forgiven. What a powerful experience this was!

I wish I could tell you that my (at the time one-year-long) affair with pornography ended that Sunday. It should have, but it didn't. I genuinely felt sorry for my lifestyle, but I did sin again with pornography. It wasn't right away, but it wasn't long before I was being defeated by pornography again. If I wasn't going to preach, then I could watch pornography any time. If I was going to preach, I wouldn't watch it the night before.

What a stupid sense of righteousness, thinking somehow timing affected the influence of my sins.

Deliverance: Finally

I experienced this torture for eleven years. I was so tired of giving in to the temptation of pornography, then feeling so guilty and unworthy to ask God's forgiveness for committing the same issue again and again. Does God get tired of forgiving me for doing the same sin over and over again? No!

In 1994, having been hired by another denomination, I became the first African American to work in their state association. After a few months, I proved to my supervisors that my position needed to be upgraded to reflect the actual work that I was doing. As a result, my title was changed to Director for Black Church Relations. I was also given a corresponding raise! Life was good!

During this year, a revival had broken out in Brownwood, Texas at the church of Dr. John Avant. Henry Blackaby joined him to travel around the country to hold meetings. Their format was this: John would retell the story of how God brought revival to him and to his church. Then Henry Blackaby would challenge people to prepare their hearts. After he prayed, he would then ask people to come to the microphone and publicly confess their sins. No music was played.

I traveled to witness one of those meetings. That moment of response was powerful. The first to respond were the teenagers. The adults soon followed the teenagers' example.

God moved my heart to confess my sin of pornography. But I didn't—the meeting ended and I was safe again.

However, the Executive Director of our state convention brought the idea back to our state office. So we held a similar time of confessing sin at our state office. A few people began to confess their sins after a time of prayer. God was speaking so loudly to my heart that I couldn't ignore Him, no matter how hard I tried. I told God, "There is no way that I'm going to confess my sin of pornography here. The white Christian community is always saying that African Americans are more immoral than other races."

Recently, I'd been involved in a conflict with a staff person about the pictures our denomination was using when it dealt with immorality. The pictures were always of African Americans and Hispanics. There I was, the only African American on staff, having to confess my sin. I fit the profile over which I had the conflict. To make things more interesting, the staff person with whom I'd argued was in the room! I didn't want to confess in this pressure arena. But God wouldn't let me off the hook.

Finally, I yielded. I got up, not knowing what to expect, thinking the worst—"I'm just fulfilling the profile." I confessed my sin of pornography publicly to this group of subordinates, peers, and superiors. To my surprise, the men surrounded me, laying their hands on me in prayer. There was no condemnation then, nor did I ever hear anything about my confession "on the grapevine" later.

There appeared to be no change of attitude toward me. Several men after the session was over told me that they too struggled with pornography. I didn't let them know it, but I was upset with them. I wished they would have publicly confessed too, so I wouldn't have been the only one.

But it didn't matter. They remained in slavery. I was free and *felt* free! The weight of all the years of lying was *finally* lifted off my back. I even felt better physically.

The hardest part of my confession wasn't over, however. I knew that I needed to go home and confess to Brenda, my wife. I left the building immediately after the session to tell Brenda, praying as I drove home. I sat her down and told her of my addiction to pornography. I told her it started before we were married, but that I hadn't been able to stop. I didn't go into a lot of detail. (Our wives don't need unnecessary baggage.) I asked for her forgiveness. She graciously forgave me. She has never asked me about it since. I am blessed to have her as a wife.

Finally, it was over. I couldn't go back to life as I had known it before. I would forever battle with pornography, but it was no longer in charge in my life! Praise God!

My public confession had brought me immediate humiliation—in the best sense of that word—and spiritual freedom from the bondage of pornography. Free at last, thank God Almighty!

Pornography Lies to You

Sexual satisfaction is the lie pornography promises but can't deliver. Many men think this satisfaction will be long-term. They don't understand the dynamics of addiction.

Pornography will please you, but it is only temporary. You can never see enough of it; thus, the addiction. Few men anticipate their bondage to pornography. This enslavement takes away any pleasure you receive to put you in a position where you are not in charge. So what begins as a little secret pleasure can be the beginning of a life of secret guilt.

Pornography is about selfishness. Pornography is about me, myself, and I. "Me-ism" is the new theology of today's postmodern culture, Christian and non-Christian alike.

Pornography is about self-deception. The deception for some is that the girl of your dreams is yours and all she wants to do is have sex with you. Through pornography, she is at your beck and call. Being in charge somehow makes you the *man* you always wanted to be or thought you should be. You feel better about yourself for the wrong reasons. Therefore, when you are not having your pornography fix, maybe you feel less self-confident and less of a man. This is wrong and Satan's lie.

You don't need to live in fantasyland to be a man. Don't focus on what you don't have, or who you think that you aren't. Focus on what you do have and those who love you just the way you are, imperfections and all. Maybe you aren't a ladies' man. You can't be anyone else, only an imitation of someone else. But no one can be a better you than you are right now!

Learn to enjoy being all you are, instead of trying to be an imitation. You are possibly missing out because you have fallen into the deception that you aren't special just the way you are. Follow your dreams, not the dreams others have for you.

A possible consequence of a pornography addiction is that you'll always be a *recovering* connoisseur of pornography. This is similar to a former alcoholic always being a recovering alcoholic. The worst place for both of these kinds of addicts is to be in places which cater to their vices.

Recovering connoisseurs of pornography must be careful of what they allow themselves to see on TV, video and at the movies. After all, addicts must learn, know and abide by their limitations. What once seemed so innocent or harmless may for some have eternal consequences. That's a heavy, but all-too-real price tag for an initial fleeting moment of pleasure.

Maybe pornography's biggest lie says that by breaking your addiction and obeying God that you'll miss out on seeing that special body. But that's saying that something can be better for you than what (or perhaps who) God has for you. This is the ultimate lie! Don't fall for it! We already know the destructiveness of pornography!

Could an Accountability Partner Help?

David Guy is one of my best friends, a former board member of my non-profit organization, and a prayer partner. Until he moved a few months ago, he was also my confidant and accountability partner who helped me stay on the right path through face-to-face meetings.

David and I would get together for breakfast after each of my trips. We'd specifically talk about women I met as I traveled. We discussed the women to whom I may have been attracted and why. We talked about any women who may have approached me. (That usually takes about five seconds—usually there are none.) We talked about my responses to those situations, and why I responded as I did.

For me, David provided peace of mind and understanding. I can admit to a guy that I have human tendencies, and that I'm not blind to a good-looking female. I don't act on my feelings, yet I believe it's important to be able to tell a trusted friend (you need only one) that I have feelings and discuss them. I can even tell him, "If I wasn't married, I would have talked to her." He listens without condemnation.

Brenda, my wife, knows that David and I meet. That being said, whenever I have been approached by a woman, I've always told Brenda. This is another step of accountability. I talk with David because Brenda doesn't need to hear all the stuff that I need to talk about. She doesn't need the burden, nor do I want Satan tempting her with lies and for her to feel that she needs to compete with other women. (I doubt if she would. She is a pretty tough lady, and we learned before we got married to be brutally honest with each other.) This style of communication is easy and works for us, but we realize that this strategy of accountability may not work for all couples. (We'll look at that aspect in greater length later.)

Pornography Impacts Your Sex Life

What if you're married and masturbating to pornography (either video, print, or in your mind) feels better than sex with your wife? (I said "if you're married" because if you're single and having sex, you shouldn't be. You are creating an entirely different set of problems for your life.) What do you do?

My addiction began before I was married. You would think that once you have the real woman with whom you can have *real* sex that the pornography addiction would end. No such luck. The pornography accompanied me into my marriage.

Within marriage, pornography can become a copout. Maybe you're not pleased with the sex in your marriage, or you want more, or you're angry with your wife. Maybe your wife is angry with you, and won't even think about sex when you're ready for it. You've decided you aren't going to have sex outside of your marriage. Does pornography offer any real benefits? Think about it: In your mind, you can have sex with a babe who is there just for you. You don't have to please her or talk to her, and it is all about you. No question like, "Was it good for you?" to worry about.

What if pornography leads you to masturbating? Masturbating is the next step while viewing or after viewing pornography. I don't know what percentage of men masturbate after being influenced by pornography, but all of the men with whom I've counseled or just talked with have gone on to masturbate. What if your masturbating is better than sex with your wife? What do you do?

If you are enjoying masturbation more than having sex with your wife, you have a problem. *First,* you should know that sex is a gift from God designed as the highest expression of love between a husband and his wife. *Second,* sexual intimacy is about giving pleasure to your spouse. Masturbation is totally about pleasing yourself. In marriage, sex is about satisfying your spouse and your spouse satisfying you. Thus, you experience the maximum sexual pleasure as you communicate to each other what you enjoy and what you don't enjoy.

Your sex life can be **improved** as you develop intimacy with your wife. Intimacy is established outside of the bed through communication. The key to mutually fulfilling sex is intimacy, which is a barometer of the closeness of the relationship. Intimacy includes sex, but it is so much more. *(Just ask your wife!)* If there are problems in the bed, it is usually because the problems outside of the bed haven't been resolved, or sometimes even discussed.

I believe as you get to *know* your wife again or maybe for the *first time* as a person specifically designed by God to be your companion for life, then one of the results will be sexual intimacy. That intimacy is much better than masturbation could ever be. Sexual intimacy requires vulnerability; masturbation doesn't. Sexual intimacy is about faith; masturbation is about control. Sexual intimacy is about serving your spouse; masturbation is about serving yourself.

What about using pornography to "get ready" for sex with your wife? Get real. Pornography probably encourages you to have sex with your wife because you get an erection from it. It has little or nothing to do with giving your wife pleasure. This is a selfish act. You are just using your wife. Without her knowing it, she becomes your unpaid prostitute.

Pornography Will Affect Your Wife

Is it my imagination or are most women always concerned about their looks, and is this why they always seem to be in front of a mirror? A woman once told me that it is hard to be a woman because when she enters any room, she always gets the *"once over,"* not just from the men, but also from the women. These women critics evaluate how well they are dressed. Passing this *"once over"* can open or shut the door to acceptance or rejection by the women in the room.

Discovering her husband is addicted to pornography can devastate a wife, causing her to feel rejected or feel less than a woman. Her possible questions: "How am I going to compete with these perfect women? How could you rather have sex with your hand than my body? What did I do wrong? If you don't find me attractive, who will?" This may send her into the bed of another man just for the affirmation that she is still attractive to someone.

One pastor's wife who found out he was a practicing homosexual went out and seduced another man. When questioned, she said, "I know it was wrong, but I needed to reassure myself that I was attractive to at least some man."

Your wife's discovery that you prefer sex with an imaginary partner may lead her to depression, and/or ultimately divorce.

Confessing Your Secret Sin to Your Wife: Yea or Nay?

Brenda is an incredibly strong woman. When praying for a wife, I prayed that she would be tough because of the nature of ministry and because of some of the specific places I believed God would take us.

When I confessed to Brenda, it wasn't because I was worried about her hearing about it from the ladies with whom I worked. I confessed to her because I didn't want anything between us. I didn't want the past to come back and surprise us: bite us in the butt. I wanted to bury my past sin once and for all. I didn't want Satan to have an opportunity to cause division between us nor any leverage over me.

As more and more men confide in me about their addiction to pornography, I'm finding that once they come clean with God, they usually desire to come clean with their wives too. Can there be a more honorable and natural motive? The man feels good because he has unloaded his burden. He is free and feels good.

But sharing this knowledge with his wife may be placing his unloaded burden on her.

More than one problem may exist with the pornography issue. First of all, it is done in secret. The man may battle it for years without the wife's knowledge. He is used to wrestling with it on his own. It is not like being married to an alcoholic or a drug addict, where the couple often works together in the fight against the addiction.

But telling your wife about your victory over pornography usually results in her immediately asking herself and you questions, such as, "How long have you been addicted to pornography? Why did you become addicted to this? Did you masturbate? If you did masturbate, did you use me just as your sex object? Why didn't you come to me for help? Why are you coming to me now?" So try to understand from her perspective the *element of surprise* she has to begin to process. You also need to understand that her method of processing may be different from yours. Most men are compartmentalized; most women are holistic. This is why most of us men can fight with our wives one moment and can want to have sex the next. But when we try to have sex with our wives immediately after a misunderstanding, she may say to us, "Don't touch me!"

Another concern after the surprise is usually a series of relationship-evaluating questions. Basically, she wants to know what went wrong, when and why. These answers run deep and may hurt both of you. These concerns/questions of surprise and the relationship are not listed in order of importance:

- What is wrong with me?
- Did I do something wrong which you felt that you couldn't talk to me about?
- How long have you been addicted to pornography?
- Did this pornography lead you into an affair?
- With whom did you or are you having, the affair?
- For how long did you have the affair?
- Is it over for good? How do you know?
- How do I know that you are telling me the truth right now?
- Can I ever trust you again? Can you be patient with me, while my trust in you is being restored?
- How can we rebuild our trust in each other again?

So should you tell your wife about your battle with, and/or victory over, pornography? There was a time when I would say without hesitation, "Yes, every man who has struggled with pornography should tell his wife about it." I no longer say this. Let me tell you why.

Last fall, in San Diego, after speaking at a *FamilyLife* Marriage Conference, I went to dinner with Bill of my prayer partners, a trial attorney, who lives there. As we discussed the possibility of writing this chapter, he said that once he asked his wife this question. He said, "Honey, I haven't done this, but if I ever had an affair and it ended, would you ever want me to tell you about it?" After thinking about his question for quite some time, she said, "No, I would never ever want to have to process such information."

It is critical that we confess our problem with pornography confidentially to someone as soon as possible. However, you may need to ask yourself if your wife needs to, wants to, or is able to process such information.

I'm not telling you that you should tell your wife, nor am I telling you not to. I am strongly recommending that you become an excellent student of your wife. You want to build her up, not tear her down.

One criterion should be the spiritual maturity of the wife and husband. You don't want your wife blaming herself for your addiction to pornography. She may feel it is her fault because she may think that she isn't *woman enough* for you; her breasts aren't big enough, she isn't pretty enough, or she isn't good in bed. Neither do you want her worrying constantly about whether or not she can trust you. Gary Smalley says that it takes the average woman **two years** for her trust to be restored once it has been broken.

After confessing my pornography addiction to the couples at this conference in San Diego, men too numerous to count shared with me how my confession gave them the courage to confess their pornography to their wives. In those cases, they felt their confessions saved their marriages.

But one husband confessed his pornography addiction to his wife and she left the conference. She had some physical issues, resulting in an unhealthy self-image. And unfortunately, this wasn't the first time this husband had confessed his pornography addiction. He asked me to write his wife. She thought he was over it and he had a relapse. Their lack of communication had both of them thinking their marriage was at one level, when it was actually at another stage. His pornography issue may have simply been a manifestation of a deeper problem.

Husbands confess their one-night stands to me. Some say they could never tell their wives, while others do.

So, I passionately encourage prayer, counsel with a godly pastor, and a consistent time of victory over pornography before taking any action. I'm not saying that there is a right and wrong answer for everyone, because everyone's circumstances as a couple are different. The issue is: "What is best for us as a couple?"

Restoring Your Relationship with God, Yourself and/or Your Wife (whether you have told her or not)

When restoring your relationship with God, *confession* is the first step. Confession is agreeing with God that indulging in pornography is wrong.

The second is *repentance*, which means to turn your back on sin. In other words, stop doing the sin! It is not about feeling sorry for your sin and then doing it again, which is what I did for eleven years. 1 John 1:9 says, "If we confess our sins, He (God) is faithful and just and will forgive us our sins and purify us from all unrighteousness."

Next, *accept God's forgiveness*. This acceptance of God's forgiveness is by faith, not feeling. You may feel relieved after confessing. That's wonderful. But you may feel the same, with no emotional change. That's all right, too. God's forgiveness is a fact, based on His integrity and character, not our emotions.

After asking God for forgiveness, *forgive yourself.* Don't listen to Satan's lie saying, "You're no good." After God's forgiveness, any negative thoughts are from Satan, not from God. Remember: fact, not feeling. Also know that God's forgiveness is complete.

What if your wife doesn't know about your pornography addiction and you don't feel it is wise for you to confess it to her? Then examine how your indulgence in pornography has created distance between the two of you. Pray about what would be the best first step toward rekindling the relationship. Think about dating your wife on a regular basis; once or twice a month would be good. Once you start, don't break it.

If you are *really* brave, ask your wife to evaluate your marriage on a one-to-ten scale. (Use "one" as the low end of the ratings and "ten" as the high end. Make sure you clarify the rating values before she answers!) If your wife says your marriage is a seven or below, ask her how can the two of you get it to a nine. Don't get defensive. Most husbands and wives have a different perspective as to the health of their marriage. Ask her what should be the first issue you as a couple need to work on. Then you, as the servant-leader, make sure that the two of you begin to consistently work on this first issue.

Whatever the specific issues for improvement are in your marriage, don't forget to pray together. It doesn't have to be a half hour of time on your knees. How about five minutes a day when neither of you is tired? There are several excellent books about couples praying together on the market, if you need that kind of jumpstart.

If you do confess your pornography to your wife, ask her the same questions about your marriage. Again, I would encourage praying and reading the Bible together. Listening and *hearing* (understanding) your wife is going to be so critical.

Your patience with her as she works through her emotional process of forgiving you and reestablishing her trust in you will take time. Don't rush her or get angry with her. Remember, you're the one with the pornography problem. She may not want to have sex with you for a while. This may be one of your toughest tests.

If she doesn't want to have sex with you for a while, don't go back to masturbating. Pray and get one close Christian male friend to pray with you and for you. If Brenda and I were counseling both of you, we would take you to 1 Corinthians 7:1-5. This passage deals with the sexual relationship between a husband and wife. Specifically, it says that in a marriage, your body belongs to your spouse. But you can't beat your wife over the head with this verse.

If you decide your marriage requires counseling, let me suggest that you pray as a couple for God to lead you to a Christian counselor who will be best for your particular situation. Try to agree together on a counselor, so the counselor isn't viewed to be on one spouse's side and against the other. Ask to speak with people this counselor has helped. If your counselor isn't using the Bible as his or her ultimate counseling authority, find another counselor. If a counselor asks you to violate biblical principles, then stop the counseling sessions immediately.

Whether you have or haven't confessed your pornography to your wife, one of the keys to restoring and/or reviving the relationship is consistency, not perfection.

Overcoming Pornography: Getting and Keeping the Victory

For me, overcoming pornography (and improving our marriage in general) was like improving my ability to jump. I hate to break the stereotype, but even though I'm an African American, I'm not an outstanding jumper. I'm good, just not outstanding.

My college basketball coach at Moody Bible Institute, Steve Irwin (not the crocodile guy), had us run and jump to try to touch the rim as part of our conditioning drills. At 5'7, I had never touched the rim. But Coach Irwin's drills conditioned me, for the first time in my life, to touch the rim! I was a happy Negro!

I went to the downtown Chicago YMCA to lift weights so I could jump higher. Coach Irwin showed me two drills specifically designed to isolate my calf muscles, which held the key to my ability to jump. One exercise was to place a board about two inches thick under the balls of my feet, then put weight on my shoulders, and squat from a standing to a sitting position. I worked out with sixty pounds on my back; and soon, I was touching the rim consistently and easily! My jumping improved about *six inches!*

Before long, I was able to (on a good wood floor) take one step and grab the rim. My increased jumping ability enabled me to block the shots of guards as tall as 6'3. A couple of times, I was able to pin the ball against the backboard. I could fly *briefly*. There were a few surprised looks as my jumping helped me to play better defense and games are won with defense!

What was amazing about my newfound ability to jump was how quickly it diminished when I went two weeks or more without lifting. So if I wanted to continue to reach those new heights, I had to keep on lifting weights on a regular weekly basis.

What does my jumping ability have to do with pornography and marriage? I believe that you have to *keep working at it.*

I have to keep in place my protections against my falling back into pornography again. I can't, and neither should you, act just by feelings. There were times I hated lifting weights, but I loved the results.

Maybe the best way to overcome pornography is to be proactive. Maybe you should consider talking to your daughter or son when they are about 10 years old. Steve Farrar recommends getting to your kids before their peers do. He thinks we should consider talking to our kids about sex by age seven (*Point Man*, p.241-248).

If your son or daughter brings the issue of pornography up, discuss it. My friend Steve said his 13-year-old son's friends exposed him to pornography. Steve's son told him about it. Steve said their conversation gave his son the freedom to talk about it to his friends, whose dads are Christians and have pornography magazines.

Safeguards for Success

Some of my **specific safeguards** against pornography include the following:

(1) I have learned to say "No" to myself about things that aren't sin for me. For example, it isn't a sin to look at a beautiful woman if she crosses your line of vision. It isn't sin to take a second and third look, but doing so doesn't make me closer to Brenda. Some of you may be saying this is lust; but unless you are mentally undressing her and committing the act with her in your mind, it likely isn't. So I don't look at other women a second or third time.

(2) As a pastor, I stopped counseling women by myself, especially after two women propositioned me.

(3) I remind myself that *I can fall*.

(4) When women, even the ones in the church, wear low-cut dresses revealing their cleavage, I now look away. In the past, it was a "freebie." I used to look, saying to myself, "It isn't my fault if they are wearing this kind of dress. They must know what they are doing and that I can see their breasts." If a woman wearing a dress showing a lot of her breasts approaches me to talk, I now just focus on her eyes and don't let my eyes wander south. It is a discipline.

(5) I also try to now look at women more as my sisters. Having three daughters also helps me in my personal war against pornography;

(6) I am actively developing a more respectful attitude toward women.

(7) I seldom go to the video store for entertainment. I had to ask myself, "Why am I always coming to the world for entertainment?" I'm not saying people should stop renting movies. I'm just saying that *I* have to be careful and not allow myself to go beyond my limitations. Seeing all those movie covers with women wearing little clothing doesn't help me at all. The urge to rent movies with nudity in them rises in me.

(8) I had to admit to myself that *I can't handle it.* I relate it to Joseph in the Bible, who was approximately 30 years old and a virgin running from Potiphar's wife. I believe he literally ran. I think if he tried to walk, he wouldn't have made it. Paul tells Timothy to *"flee"* from lust. My nature is not to change channels if I see nudity or the potential for it, but I do change it because I don't want to revert to my former situation. For some it might require canceling your local TV cable. It may require unplugging the TV in your hotel room when you travel. I often stay with friends

when I'm traveling because of the rich fellowship and another source of accountability and protection regarding pornography. It may mean not going to certain movies on "Boys Night Out."

(9) I have secured a male accountability partner to meet with on a weekly or bi-monthly basis. Maybe more than anything else, these partners help you keep an attitude which leads you to the action of saying, "No" to anything which may move you toward falling back into the pornography trap.

(10) I try to keep myself out of situations that are dangerous for me.

Saying "No" the first time can be the hardest, but the more you say "No," the easier it becomes and you gain more freedom and control over your addiction.

What if you have a relapse? Tell your accountability partner. It is not the end of the world. In learning to walk, most babies fall many times before they master walking. The critical issue isn't how many times you fall; it is getting up after every fall. God will always forgive you. He's the one that suggested forgiving "seventy times seven." Don't give in to Satan's lie that you will never get it right. God doesn't stop loving us, even if we fail. He's waiting to celebrate our victories with us, and more of them every day!

Don't let the enemy use your struggle as a means to discourage you about your walk with God. He can't take you from the Father. In John 10:28-30 Jesus said, "I give them eternal life, and they shall never perish; *no one can snatch them* out of My hand. My Father, who has given them to Me, is greater than all; *no one can snatch them* out of my Father's hand. I and the Father are one." Romans 8:37-39 reads, "No, in all these things we're more than conquerors through Him who loved us. For I am convinced that neither death nor life, neither angels nor demons, neither the present nor the future, nor any powers, neither height nor depth, nor anything else in all creation (this includes Satan), will be able to separate us from the love of God that is in Christ Jesus our Lord."

Don't compare yourself with others you may know who are also trying to break the cycle of their pornography addiction. We're not in competition with anyone.

Every day, I must say "No" to pornography. Another preventative step is praying with Brenda daily. We don't pray about pornography, we praise God for who He is, for our girls, each other, family, friends, and for events of the specific day. Praying with Brenda reinforces my commitment to her and the girls.

What kind of legacy am I going to leave is the question that helps me fight pornography's lure. Every man should see The Big Picture. We have to look beyond our present momentary pleasure to the consequences of our actions. Galatians 6:7, 8 is clear about this: "Do not be deceived; God cannot be mocked. A man reaps what he sows. The one who sows to please his sinful nature, from that nature will reap destruction; the one who sows to please the Spirit, from the Spirit will reap eternal life."

Do we really want to reap the fruit of pornography? I don't think so.

Last, but certainly not least is my relationship with Christ. God has been, and continues to be, so good to my family, me, and the ministry He has given me. I don't want to lose it. Pornography certainly isn't worth the risk. To me, there is nothing like walking with God as He develops the intimacy between the two of us. The last couple of years, He has been teaching me and exposing me to so much, I don't want to jeopardize that by a short momentary pleasure whose long-term goal is to destroy my family and me.

This is walking by faith, not by feeling. It is the freedom not to be controlled by anyone or anything but God, who loved and loves us so much that He allowed His own Son, Jesus Christ, to die for our sins, so that we could have eternal fellowship with Him!

A Word to Wives

I've discovered that quite a few women read my books for men, which I think is commendable. Ladies, you are investing in your marriage. As you have read this chapter, you may be wondering if your husband is wrestling with pornography. May I suggest that you not ask him about it, but pray for him instead? Maybe your prayer should be: "Dear Lord, if my husband is involved in pornography, would your Holy Spirit convict him that this is wrong and move him to confess his sin and quit this destructive sin? Will you please forgive him and give me your strength to forgive him and not hold a grudge against him? Lord, help me not to unintentionally act differently towards him. Help us to discuss it so I may help him so he won't have a relapse."

Ladies, if you should ask your husbands if they are involved with pornography, I ask you to be willing to forgive them immediately, with no resentment. I'm not justifying their actions. But you must understand they are becoming vulnerable to you. If this happens, it is time for reconciliation. Your actions here may help serve as another accountability motivation because your husbands don't want to lose you.

These are merely some of my prayerful suggestions. Please listen to the Holy Spirit.

A Final Reflection

Let me say a word about my deliverance from my pornography addiction. It is not the norm, according Christopher McCluskey, a Christian sex therapist: "The vast majority of men have had to seek Christian counseling and participate in a support group for men with this struggle because the addiction is usually much more than the simple lure of naked women."

"Men can so easily 'sexualize' their emotional needs and seek to meet all of their legitimate and emotional needs through sexual fulfillment. There is a real healing and maturing process that needs to occur for these men—they are stunted at an adolescent level of psychological development and are usually incapable of connecting with a woman on a healthy, intimate level until they do this work, even if they do stop using pornography.

"Their use of pornography and masturbation is usually just the tip of the iceberg—the real struggle is not the lure of sexual temptation, although it is HUGE all by itself; but it's all the other emotional baggage wrapped up in their misuse of their sexuality."

This therapist is saying that there is often more to the addiction besides resisting the temptation and stopping the destructive behavior. The motivation of the behavior must be healed.

So please don't feel guilty or unspiritual if your addiction doesn't end in the way mine did. Whether you are healed by God all at once or through counseling and a support group, it doesn't matter. Let me encourage you that you can be delivered through the grace of God. Seek Him and His healing power.

Action Points
Chapter Eight
Kiss of Death: The Secret Sin of Pornography

1. What are the most common places in which you encounter pornography? How can you avoid pornography in those places?

2. How do you think pornography could hurt your marriage?

3. How do you think your wife would respond if she discovered you were addicted to pornography?

4. How would you respond if you discovered your wife was addicted to pornography?

5. How have—or will—you tell your children to deal with pornography?

6. What would the impact on your marriage be if your wife discovered you were masturbating more often than making love to her?

7. What would the impact on your marriage be if you discovered your wife was masturbating more often than making love to you?

8. What limits have you set for yourself regarding pornography?

9. Do you have a friend who will keep you accountable regarding sexual purity? If not, who is a likely candidate?

10. Are you willing to pray specifically for your pastor(s), your family, your friends and yourself to be sexually pure? Schedule three times this week to do exactly that.

Chapter Nine
Pastoral Marriages: Pastors Are Humans, Too!

Marriage is a wonderful blessing and gift of God to men, to women, to their children and to the people who know them. Many of us know that marriage has changed our lives for the better.

Those of us who have the additional blessing of being in ministry know the additional pressure and struggle of being married (and perhaps having children) in a ministry context. Some of you are having a blast as you are able to balance marriage, family, and ministry. And some others of you love your marriage, family and the ministry God has given you, but you are having some difficulty with balancing these three. Hopefully, your spouse is your best friend in either case—because especially in ministry, you need to keep your spouse as your best friend.

Blessings of a Pastoral/Ministry Marriage

Pastoral marriages are similar to non-ministerial ones in that God intended for most people to be married (Genesis 2:18-24), and that includes those engaged in ministry. Yet there are some pastoral/ministry marriage issues that deserve special attention.

A *common calling to serve* is vital in pastoral/ministry marriages. In order to experience God's blessings for a pastoral marriage, it is critical for both spouses to know that they both have been called into ministry by the Lord. It doesn't matter whether one is the pastor or they are co-pastors. But when *both* husband and wife have understood and accepted God's call into ministry, it opens the door for them to experience at least some of the fruit of the Spirit (Galatians 5:22, 23), specifically *peace* and *joy*. This acceptance of God's call into ministry doesn't mean that both will be in direct ministry to the public. It does mean, however, that both accept that one or both of them has a public responsibility. This understanding usually results in peace and joy in a marriage from "oneness."

Another blessing of a ministerial marriage is that *children* of these marriages often ask Jesus Christ into their lives at an earlier age than those who aren't, especially if Dad and Mom have a consistently good relationship with Christ and each other. Through God's grace, our three girls all accepted Christ before or by the age of seven.

Clear and understandable communication with God and each other is vital in every Christian marriage, but this aspect tends to become magnified in a pastoral/ministry marriage: First, *you must pray and read God's Word together.* Yes, you both still need personal time alone with God. But your calling to ministry is shared. Your life as man and wife is shared. So at least some of your time before God and in the Word needs to be shared, too.

Second, your marriage should provide a *built-in accountability system where both spouses listen to each other.* This requires blocking out time and guarding that time for you to talk to each other daily, and not just about the weather. And *you must listen to each other's advice.* This requires four things of you:

•That you get along;

•That you trust each other;

•That you respect each other; and

•That you be consistent—don't be one way at church and another at home. This can be devastating to a spouse and even more so for children.

Following up on this last point, it is critical that you *practice what you preach* or your children and congregation will learn how to be hypocrites. A consistently good (not perfect) marriage and family life will give credibility to your sermons and ministry. Paul didn't miss making this point to his protégé:

"[The pastor or leader] must manage his own family well and see that his children obey him with proper respect. If anyone does not know how to manage his own family, how can he take care of God's church?" (1 Timothy 3:4,5)

You, your spouse and your children (if you have any) must have *a place of refuge* from the ministry. The ministry family seldom has a place of refuge where they aren't "on" all the time. I wonder if this is why people so often say that preachers' children are so bad. Ministry families need rest like all families do. Preachers' children are under *tremendous* pressure to be perfect along with their parents! We need to remove that pressure at home.

So it makes sense that *each spouse should make the home a sanctuary for the other* away from the ministry. This can happen if our priorities are in biblical order:

•God;
•Your spouse;
•Your children; and then
•The ministry (1 Timothy 3:4,5).

Pastors and spiritual leaders getting these priorities out of order set themselves up to experience the destructive consequences of such a poor choice. Be careful not to allow the ministry to become your other lover, allowing the ministry to become more important than your spouse.

Don't seduce yourself into thinking that the ministry can't function without you. Learn to say, "No," and learn to delegate. If you don't have the staff, teach a layperson. If you don't have either, ask God to send you someone. The late Dr. T.B. Maston once told me, "You know that the Lord did okay before you got here and He will probably do okay after you leave." He was basically telling me to slow down because I couldn't do everything.

You and your spouse need time away to be refreshed and hear from God. It is difficult to hear from God when you are burned out. Your ministry also needs a periodic break from you too. No time off can lead to burnout. My friend and life coach, Bruce Gordon, former president of Focus on the Family Canada and speaker for FamilyLife Canada says that he and Denise (his wife) take time off from ministry. They find this time off essential to the health of their God-given ministry effectiveness.

A dear friend of mine, who is presently working for a parachurch ministry, told me that once he had had an affair. I assumed he was talking about a woman. My assumption was wrong: He told me the affair was with the church he formerly pastored. He said that it cost him his first marriage and profoundly affected one of his children. When we had this conversation, he was in his second marriage to a beautiful woman. Two years later, he was preparing for his third marriage. He misses the pastorate, but having his responsibilities to his marriage, family, and ministry out of balance may have, for him, ended any opportunities for pastoring again.

Somebody's Watching You

Pastoral marriages are fishbowl relationships. Singles, children, youth, young and old married couples, non-Christians, other pastors, and the entire community are watching your marriage. Face it: More people than you realize are evaluating your marriage.

The reality of life is that no marriage is perfect because neither spouse is. Not even the marriages of those in ministry are exempt from imperfection. Sometimes circumstances— some within our control, others beyond our control—can creep into our marriages. These circumstances create hurdles for married couples to jump. The good news is that we have the perfect Holy Spirit living in us to help us clear those hurdles.

While serving as interim pastor for a church where the pastor had been fired for drug use and sexual immorality, one thing I didn't realize was how closely people in the congregation and community of this small town were watching my marriage.

This was brought to my attention on two occasions. One was when a single young lady who wanted to get married said, "The sermon which has impacted me the most is the one Brenda and you live. Your marriage, how you treat each other, blesses me. I want the kind of marriage the two of you have." To that point, I'd never thought of people watching us as a couple!

The other instance was when one of the associate pastors stepped out of the pulpit while I was preaching! I had just said, "if you are a preacher and you and your spouse are having major marital problems, you don't need to be in the pulpit until you get your problems resolved." To my surprise, one of my favorite associate ministers in this church calmly got up and went and sat on the front pew!

When I agreed to serve as interim pastor, the first thing I publicly told the congregation was this: "If my wife or family needs me at the same time someone in the congregation or if the entire congregation needs me, I'll be with my wife and children." I based this statement on the 1 Timothy passage discussed earlier. Remember, it asks how a man can manage the house of God if he can't manage his own household well. It seems to imply that home comes before ministry. In fact, one's home life qualifies or disqualifies one from ministry. Unknowingly, my statement forced the ministers, deacons, lay leaders and men in general to reevaluate their relationship with their wives and families. The statement set a tone for integrity in ministry.

Two years later, the associate pastor who stepped out of the pulpit said, "Your statement forced me to work with my wife to resolve the problems we were having. Now, I'm pastoring with her full support. Thank you."

It is funny when I look back at that time. Brenda and I had been married only two years when we began pastoring this church. I had no idea of the mistakes I was making with her. We certainly didn't have a perfect marriage (and still don't), but we had a healthy one. These poor people, who were starving for the Word of God, weren't seeing any healthy marriages to imitate, either.

How and Why Some Ministerial Marriages Get In Trouble

We have already mentioned that giving the ministry first place in your life is a recipe for disaster.

Divorce is often the wrong, but all-too-natural consequence. When people talk about divorce on the grounds of irreconcilable differences, it causes me to smile inwardly. It is not that I take divorce lightly. It is just that I believe God has a sense of humor. He made men and women so different that every marriage has irreconcilable differences.

For example, men and women use the same words, but certainly don't use them in the same way. It's as though we don't even speak the same language. Men and women don't speak the same amount of words during a 24-hour period. Men and women approach things differently, such as shopping. Many men know what they want, go buy it and go home. For many women, shopping is an adventure! If it takes all day, it's okay. Driving all over town to find the best sale, even though they may burn up their savings in gas, is fine with them. For some men, watching a TV sports event on Sunday afternoon can become a religion that their wives don't understand.

That's just the beginning of the differences many couples carry into their marriages. Would it help to know that there are reasons for those differences that can be traced back to the differences in the needs of women and men? According to *FamilyLife*, the five basic needs of men and women are different:

for Men	*for Women*
1. Sexual fulfillment	1. Affection
2. Recreational companionship	2. Conversation
3. An attractive spouse	3. Honesty & openness
4. Domestic support	4. Financial support
5. Admiration	5. Family commitment

Not knowing or understanding how and why your spouse is different can lead to small problems, which may later grow into major problems if not dealt with biblically.

Trust issues are at the core of any relationship. Some African American couples still deal with the negative affects of slavery on trust. Slavery often pitted slave men and women against each other, thus damaging the trust factor in male-female relationships and family systems. This lack of trust can be (and has been) passed on from one generation to the next. Sometimes, these negative roots penetrate the surface of a marriage. When coupled with those extra pressures of a ministry, marriage can be uniquely difficult for African American couples.

Regardless of their backgrounds, some couples get in trouble because they don't unload their baggage of pain from past experiences. Others bring misinformation about sex into the marriage. Still others don't understand servant-leadership, what it means to be a biblical head of the house, or what submission is supposed to be about. Some men think that headship means dictatorship. This misinformation has produced severe consequences for some couples, even leading some of them into abusive situations.

Contrary to the results weight training can produce in the gym, carrying extra baggage in a marriage usually weakens the relationship. So how can we avoid that baggage in pastoral/ministry marriages? Let's take a closer look at the key issues we face.

The Calling of Husband and Wife to Ministry

One of the first issues ministerial couples face is the call to ministry. When one spouse is initially called into official ministry he or she seldom waits—or even understands the need to wait—for God to call their spouse into the role of supporting of this call.

Here, timing can be everything. Without waiting for a spouse to sense the common call, the result is that the spouse who doesn't feel called may feel *forced* into the ministry. This *new, forced,* and *public* position may result in this spouse resenting their spouse who is in ministry, the congregation, and sometimes even God Himself. If there are children, they may also be affected negatively by the tension and frustration of their parents as they work through this situation.

If one spouse feels "forced" into the ministry, it will hinder the effectiveness of the other in ministry. Remember, the congregation does not know or understand the demands on a ministerial couple:

- Isolation/loneliness,
- Limited time with their spouse
- Raising their children in a fishbowl
- Traveling, speaking, writing as your God-given ministry grows
- High expectations of congregations
- High expectations of their spouse
- Your own high expectations you place on yourself for ministry "success"
- The increasing perception of needing to work more and more outside of the home with inadequate vacation time and finances
- Cell phone intrusions

What Happens When the Wife is the Pastor?

Last year, while speaking at the Leadership Conference held at Calvary Revival Church in Norfolk, Virginia, several women pastors expressed a problem with their husbands in regards to their ministry. They said that they felt that their husbands were struggling with them being pastors. I asked them to explain.

One woman replied, "After church is over, my husband goes and sits in the car when all the people surround me at the altar."

I asked, "What do you want him to do?"

She answered, "I want him to be with me at the altar, publicly supporting me."

I continued with a more delicate question. "How did you accept your call? Did you and your husband discuss it and pray about or on one Sunday did you respond in a church service on your own?"

Her guilt caused her to drop her head. She said regretfully, "I didn't discuss it with him. I responded publicly. I know it surprised him."

"As the man, he may not have known what to do. He may have needed time to work through some issue, or he may have wanted the opportunity to work through these issues with you privately before it became public," I said. I sensed these were things she had wondered about but never confirmed even with a friend, much less her husband. "Discussing it ahead of time would have helped him to know how to respond publicly, especially if his partners were teasing him about you accepting your call.

"It may have hurt him too. He may not resent your call, but your response to your call may have demonstrated a lack of respect for him as your head in the context of your marriage. This could even make it difficult for him to listen to your sermons, if he feels there is inconsistency." (Men, our wives can feel the same way about how we pursued our own calls to ministry.)

This reminder of our fragile male egos, the headship of her husband in their marriage, and the simple need to talk over major life decisions with your spouse made sense to this precious sister in Christ. I asked her if her husband loved her.

She said, "Very much so."

"Is he supportive of you as pastor?"

She said, "He is extremely supportive."

I suggested, "Consider apologizing to him for not discussing your call to ministry with him before you accepted it publicly. Then pray about asking him to stand with you after church because you want his support and the security it brings you. Then the two of your pray about all that we have discussed." I paused before asking, "What do you think about these suggestions?"

She said, "God has confirmed what you have said in my heart."

"Your husband may have simply not known what the correct 'church response' to your new position was, or if there was one."

With much fear and trembling, let me share another observation. When there is confusion in the home about whether the father or the mother is the head of the family, the children can easily experience gender confusion. God uses the man not only to help boys determine their masculinity, but also for girls to realize their feminity.

Investing in Your Marriage

Continue to date your spouse.

I know you've read this before, but I want you to get it. Date at least once a month. Go on your dates without your children. If you go to see a movie, go to see the movie first, then have dinner or dessert or coffee or all three. Don't talk business, but talk and listen to each other.

If you are a man, don't try to fix any of your wife's problems she shares with you, unless she asks you for advice. Somehow, listening to her issues without trying to solve them provides security for some women. I don't understand it either, but we don't have to. Just do it!

Call your spouse every now and then during the day to let your spouse know you are thinking about them.

Pray and spend time in the Word together on a regular basis. Make sure your life in ministry is consistent with your life at home. Realize that your marriage will always require a willingness to grow.

Once a year, attend some kind of marriage enrichment. Today's options include

- *FamilyLife Weekend to Remember*
- *Billy Graham School of Evangelism: Balancing Marriage/Family & Ministry*
- *Building Lasting Relationships: Marriage Seminar*
- *Marriage Encounter*
- *Life Advance Marriage Seminars*
- Or, your local church may have a family/marriage enrichment seminar.

Pastoral Marriages Have Enemies

In the early 1980's, when I was serving as a Home Missionary in Oklahoma, I heard Dr. James Dobson share an unnerving experience. He said that he was on a plane and the woman beside him was praying. After she finished her prayer, he commended her on praying in public. She said, "I'm not praying to who you think I am. I'm member of the Church of Satan. Our entire church is praying for Christian leaders to fall, especially in the area of sexual immorality."

Their prayers and efforts are working. All you have to do is look at the number of Christian leaders who have fallen in the area of sexual immorality since the mid-80s through today.

What can we do to protect our marriages?

Protecting Your Marriage

At the Promise Keepers' Pastors Conference in Atlanta in 1996, Coach Bill McCartney's said that 70% of pastors were guilty of inappropriate behavior with women.

Before I got married and even several years after I was married, I counseled women regardless if they were single or married. To me, it was no big deal. I wasn't going to commit adultery.

Two experiences forever changed my position on this.

I was scheduled to counsel a woman who was having serious and legitimate marriage problems. I knew her husband. She and her husband were wealthy. I was working from home that day and she was to meet me there at noon. Something told me to have Brenda, who was a city librarian, come home for lunch about the same time. It wasn't a minute before Brenda came in the house that this woman, whose wedding ring could pay for our house, propositioned me.

I was shocked and scared at the same time! I was so glad Brenda walked in the room just seconds later. Brenda, who trusts me, said, "I'm so sorry. I didn't know that you were counseling. I can leave and let you two keep talking." I told her that she didn't need to go. A few minutes later, the woman left. I immediately told Brenda what happened. We were both in shock for a few days.

Sometimes, I'm a little slow in catching on. Another test came my way in a few days. When Dr. Gary Chapman led me to Christ as a teenager, he lit a passion in me for discipleship as he discipled me. After watching my home church explode over the years as it discipled its members, I decided to do the same for the church I had planted and stayed on to pastor.

One day, I was delivering the discipleship workbooks we were going to use to those who were going to participate. I called one woman to let her know I would be dropping books off for her and her husband, both good friends of ours, about twenty minutes later. When I arrived at their house and knocked on the door, I heard a voice saying, "Come on in."

I didn't think twice (stupid me!). I entered the house and waited in the hallway, near the stairway. All of a sudden, this beautiful woman begins to make her way down the stairs, wearing a see-through intimate woman's garment. She asked me, "Do you see anything you want?"

My mind was racing like crazy. "Here I am, an African American pastor with this half-dressed blue-eyed blonde woman! What is she trying to do to me? If I have sex with her, I'm dead. If I offend her by not having sex with her, all she has to do is say that I did and I'm dead."

I was Joseph with Potiphar's wife. How could I back out of this situation, and fast? I asked for a glass of water to try to collect myself. I wanted to appear that I wasn't surprised by her outfit. After a few gulps of water, I told her I was running late, which was true, and that the next person was expecting me, which was also true. She seemed to accept my reasons and I left.

Once I got in my car, I broke into a big sweat. There was still no guarantee that she wouldn't lie about what did and didn't happen. I called Vince, one of the elders of the church, and told him about it. I remember asking him, "Why would a woman wear see-through clothing to answer her door when I was delivering a *discipleship* book to her and her husband?"

Vince gave me an answer I'll never forget. He said, "Power. You represent power in the pulpit. You often say 'No' to some of these women, who are used to walking over their husbands. You're safe. You're married. You are the preacher. You're forbidden fruit. This makes you attractive. Who are you going to tell if you have an affair? What excuse could you possibly give for having an affair? The reasons go on and on."

Vince protected me, by making me aware when a woman in our church was acting inappropriately towards me. He saw what I didn't.

These two incidents ended my counseling women alone—or even being in situations with women alone.

Balancing Marriage/Family & Ministry

How can you honestly tell when your relationships with your spouse and children are out of balance with your ministry/work responsibilities?

Let's start here: *Are you always bringing work home? Are you too busy to play with your spouse and/or family?* If you're too busy to play with your spouse and children, then you are too busy!

Presently, I'm trying to write this book and another book proposal this summer. The easiest way to do this is for me to leave home for a few days to focus and get it done. But my girls are out of school for the summer. They have a developed a passion for basketball this summer. So I'm writing around their schedule because I want them to know that they are much more important to me than anything that I could ever write.

The best time for me to write is in the mornings when I'm most creative, but the best time for us to get a gym when it isn't so crowded for basketball is around 8 a.m.

I'm spending time in the Bible with my girls and giving them some one-on-one time. They are teaching me a lot as they are physically changing from girls to young women! Sometimes, they give me more information than I care to process. I try to spend more time in the Word with my girls, especially during the summer. For some down time I go with them to the movies. I have all girls, so I see a lot of "chick" flicks. Pray for me.

Another indicator that you are out of balance is if you are stressed out, easily upset or angry. How are you communicating at work on days other than Sunday? Are you encouraging, positive, demanding, negative? What would your family say? What would your co-workers say?

When I worked for a Christian ministry, it was such a stressful job that I would come home, go to my bedroom and not come out for an hour. I traveled more than sixty thousand air miles a year. Christian and non-Christian doctors said that the Christian organization which I worked for was the most stressful place to work in the city.

One day, my family and I got in our van to go somewhere. One of my daughters asked Brenda, "Mom, is Dad going with us?" I was right there in the car, yet my daughter didn't ask me, she asked my wife.

I had become a "ghost dad." (I heard the term on an Oprah show on fathers. My wife made me watch this particular show.)

If you shudder and have guilt pangs just by hearing the words "ghost dad"—which is how I responded—you may be one. So what can you do about it?

Give your family priority in your schedule. Slot them in for the time they need, and keep those appointments. Brenda and I coordinate a *Family & Ministry Calendar* for that very reason. The family calendar has all the girls' and Brenda's events scheduled, so I can schedule my ministry events around theirs. Our family calendar has priority over my ministry calendar.

This was tremendous when it was only theory. The challenge came when the first "big" ministry event came up. After these calendars were in place for a few months, I was asked to go to Zimbabwe to minister. Before I could give my answer, I knew that I had to check our family calendar. Our family had agreed that we would always spend Spring Break together. The question was, "Would the Zimbabwe trip come during Spring Break?" If it did, I couldn't go. If not, I was home free. The trip wasn't during Spring Break, so I could go. It meant a lot to my girls that I would rather be with them than overseas.

This summer, I wasn't traveling between mid-May until the end of August. An invitation came for me to attend the *African American Healthy Marriage Initiative Roundtable Discussion.* The event was convened by the Centre for New Black Leadership, Executive Directors Association of OIC of America, and Alpha Phi Alpha Fraternity, Inc. in partnership with the U.S. Department of Health & Human Services Administration for Children and Families. Twenty-five African Americans, Christian and non-Christian, were invited. This was huge, and the government was paying for it!

I shared the invitation with Brenda so we could discuss it. She insisted that I go and cancel local meetings. She said, "You've been working out with the girls every day and you will miss only two days of their basketball camp. Go." What a wonderful woman!

I left the decision in her hands, and Brenda encouraged me to go because I had made "family deposits"—time and energy clearly focused on her and our daughters— all summer. Therefore, she felt I could "withdraw" some of those deposits. Remember, no deposits in—no withdrawals. Too often marriage partners seek to make withdrawals, when they have not made any deposits, often resulting in frustration and conflict.

Another way I've tried to protect and invest in my marriage and family is to *have regular and consistent time with family.* Last year, I traveled about 100,000 miles. What I do on short trips is to take each of my girls, one-on-one with me, if they are caught up in school and are behaving well. I use my frequent flyer miles to cover their travel costs.

For example, once I spoke to the Miami Dolphins in New Orleans. Whenever Christina sees me watching a football game being played in the Super Dome, she'll come in the room and say, "Daddy, remember when we were there together?" She'll never forget our time together. It is priceless! Granted, you don't get much rest when you take your children with you. In my case, I speak, then, I try to keep up with a 13- or 14-year-old. But you are creating memories and a legacy.

Brenda and I also take the girls with us when we can on some of our marriage retreats and make short vacations after the marriage retreat is over. Last summer was probably our best summer as a family. Our marriage ministry had Brenda and me on both coasts. We took the girls with us.

Speaking of that, when it is appropriate, why not take the children with you to emergencies or crisis situations? That way they'll have a better understanding what and why you do what you do. They also can pray more specifically for you when they can't go with you. They gain a priceless understanding which lessens the competition between them and ministry for your time.

There are other benefits in this practice. Once I took my girls with me to do a hospital visitation (secure permission before you do this). At the end of our visit with a dear saint, I had one of the girls pray for her recovery. Then the other two girls prayed. The woman was so blessed, and so were the girls. So was I.

The Pastoral/Ministry Safeguards Checklist

In review, here are some practical safeguards for protecting any marriage, especially a pastoral or other ministry marriage:

1. Pray with your spouse daily.
2. Have family devotions at least weekly.
3. Pray with your children at least weekly.
4. Pray for them daily.
5. Eat one meal together daily—everyone gets to talk, maybe read a chapter out of the Bible a day—no phones are answered during this time and no TV.
6. Take at least one day off a week, and *guard it.*
7. Play hard with your family.
8. Have an accountability partner.
9. Have prayer partners praying for you and your family daily.
10. If you are pastoring a church, encourage your congregation to pray for you.
11. Take some time away from everyone, maybe a day or two quarterly, just to get refreshed and hear from God.
12. Every few months, give your spouse three days to a week away from her responsibilities, you and the kids—especially if your spouse is a stay-at-home mom. She may never ask for it, but she is always taking care of somebody and she needs time just for her. If she is away, she doesn't have to worry about meals, clothes, a clean kitchen, etc. You can clean the kitchen and the house the day before she gets back. She'll never know unless the kids talk. Threaten the kids.
13. Develop a healthy respect for your enemy, who is actively at work to cause you to fall.

14. Men, don't be by yourself with a woman other than your wife if at all possible. Ladies, don't be by yourself with a man other than your husband if at all possible.

15. Realize that you **can fall sexually.**

16. Be careful what you let your eyes see.

17. Be careful how you touch those of the opposite gender.

18. Never assume that because someone's a member of your church that they share your concern for keeping your marriage healthy.

19. Don't counsel someone of the opposite gender by yourself. Have your spouse with you to bring the opposite gender's perspective and support to the session.

20. Avoid the appearance of evil. Period.

21. Work through conflict, don't avoid it. In my first book, *Your Wife Can Be Your Best Friend,* I describe the rules of "fighting fair" in marriage. Whether you use my book or not, I suggest a couple make and agree on rules to work through conflict. Conflict is reality, so to avoid conflict is to attempt to avoid reality.

22. Don't break your family dates with your spouse or your children unless there's a real emergency, like somebody dying. Train your staff or lay leadership to serve in your place to cover for you during scheduled family time.

23. Turn off cell phone during your date.

Do You Have A Vision For Your Family?

In the secular world and in the Christian community, it is common for people to write personal mission statements.

Let me encourage you to encourage every member of your family to write a *personal mission statement.* Then write a *family mission statement.* I got this idea from the Southern

Baptists, who have a family evangelism program. It is pretty good.

In writing a family mission statement, everyone who can talk intelligently (I know this may be a tough call for some) is to have input. Try to develop a statement that answers these three questions:

- •Who are we, as a family, going to be for Christ?
- •What will make us distinctive as a Christian family?
- •What practical things will help us toward those
        objectives?

I'm not giving our family mission statement as an example here because I don't want to influence yours. I will, however, share a couple things that are in it.

One, we don't accept phone calls during dinnertime. There is no TV allowed during this time (This kills me sometimes because I live in the Mountain Standard Time zone. A lot of the East Coast games start while I'm eating dinner.) We usually will read one chapter of the Bible at dinner, which may result in a 20-minute discussion or no discussion, or just a lot of laughing. But you get the idea. These rules are just for dinner. There are others for the house.

Your personal and family mission statements should complement each other. They should give direction and boundaries for your family. Both statements should be biblically based. They both should make it easier to make personal and family decisions and should help each member of the family to say "No" to things which don't fit with these statements. They should also slow your life down a little.

My prayer for all of you who are married and are in full-time ministry is that you will take steps, if you haven't already, to protect your marriage. Then you can experience all the blessings that God intended for you and your family to have.

Your marriage, family and the ministry God has given you can be tremendous blessings—*and* you can keep your spouse as your best friend.

Questions to Consider
Chapter Nine
Pastoral Marriages: Pastors are Humans, too!

1. In a perfect world, what would a balance between your marriage, family, and the ministry look like for you? Write it out, then ask your wife and children separately. Do you all have the same picture in mind? Why or why not?

2. How can you tell, or can't you discern, when responsibilities are getting out of balance for you? Are you in denial?

3. How does your wife and/or children let you know that you are out of balance or do you even hear them?

4. How do you or can you get things back in balance?

5. What do you do to relax? When is the last time you really relaxed?

6. How do you play? When do you play?

7. Do you have a day off? If you don't have a day off, you are too busy and you are burning out. Remember, even the Lord took a day off.

8. How would your family answer these questions?

9. Do you have a Family Calendar? Can your family and you create one and give it priority over the ministry?

10. When will your family and you sit down to create your family calendar and your day off?

11. Are members of your congregation commenting positively to your spouse or you about your marriage? Are single people saying that they want a marriage like yours? Why or why not?

Chapter Ten
Making This Your Last Marriage

Brenda and I continue to become more and more involved with preserving the institution of marriage by partnering with *The Billy Graham Schools of Evangelism, FamilyLife Marriage Conferences, The African American Healthy Marriage Initiative* of the U.S. Department of Health and Human Services, and our own marriage seminar ministry— *Building Lasting Relationships.* Brenda and I desire to help couples make their marriages mutually fulfillingl. We continually are introduced to more couples who are in their second, third or more marriages, most of whom are usually struggling trying to make their present marriage their last one. Brenda and I can see their desire to stay committed to each other and we can see their fear of another martial failure.In meeting these couples, my concern for their marriage survival rises because statistics prove that once a person gets divorced, the odds are 80% that he/she will remarry and that 60% of these second marriages will also end in divorce. So when a person divorces, it seems that that person is headed for at least two divorces and possibly at least three marriages.

While some folks condemn them for being divorced in the first place, I think (right or wrong) some things are hard, if not impossible, to undo. So my agenda isn't judging or condemning people who have been in multiple marriages. My desire is to help them, no matter how many marriages they have been in, to make their present marriage their last one.

Real People

I've asked some couples who are like family to me and who have been involved in more than one marriage or long-term relationship to allow me to interview them as to what they are doing to make their present marriage their last one.

You will hear from three couples. Two of the men are in their third marriage, one is in his second one. Two of the women are in their second marriage and one is in her first marriage after being in a relationship for nine years. The length of their marriages ranges from three to eighteen years. You may relate to their struggles and their victories may provide practical marriage survival tips. Their relationships will bless you hearts and give you hope. And I strongly believe that if some of you put some of their principles into practice, they may very well save your marriage.

Rich & Kaye

The first couple has been married for approximately three years. It is his third marriage and her second. Here is their interview:

Question: What are some of the things you want to do differently to make this your last marriage?

Rich:

Kaye emphasized that one of the most crucial issues in marriage is communicating, which is something I'm learning. I've never communicated well and probably don't do as well now as I could, but listening to Kaye, I can better appreciate what it is she's saying. First you communicate, whether good orbad, that there is a problem, then how you feel about it.

For example, let's say what you want to see and what your partner, your best friend, wants to see is different. You've communicated how you feel. Now, do I desire to do something about it? After I decide that, then I think about the trustworthiness and honesty of my partner. Trust is looking to the future and the honesty is looking toward the past. If they were honest in the past, you trust they will be honest in the future. And then the effort: How much effort do I want to put into doing something about this problem?

Question: Kaye, you said communication is critical to you. Rich stated that you helped him in this area. Can you give an example of ways you felt he wasn't communicating with you early in your relationship?

Kaye:

Rich doesn't like conflict. We both come from past experiences of being an enabler. We both want peace so in order to avoid conflict we just say, "Oh, that'll be fine." I have to trust that Rich really believes *that's fine*. Well, the truth of the matter is that he didn't even think about some things. He just said "That's fine" because it was easier for him than discussing it. For example, I might ask,"Do you want to go to a Broncos game or a concert?" He'll say, "That's fine, whatever you want." Of course I want to go to the concert, so I get tickets and we go. I might hear later, "Gee, I really wish I'd seen that Broncos game." It is the kind of thing when you come in and say, "That's fine," without believing you can express your real needs or desires.

One of the reasons I fell in love with Rich was because he raised his two daughters and I saw the respect they had for him. When you are a woman marrying a man, you need to look at the relationships, besides ex-wives, he has established with other women in his life: his sister, daughters, friends' wives. I saw the respect, love and trust with them. With his daughters, since it had been just the three of them, they would say we are going to do something and he would say "That's fine" without asking if it was okay with me. Even though they were adults and not living here, when they were visiting, it was important for him to communicate first with me and to see if that fit in and how the two of us were going to be parents to these two girls.

Question: Rich, is it fair to say that you did not want to deal with conflict?

Rich:

Yes, I am that way everywhere. If I find myself in a disagreement with someone, I try to explain my perspective. If they keep shooting me down, I'll just walk away. I think it's okay to disagree with someone as long as the dialogue is healthy. But if they won't listen, I walk away. Even my daughter knows if I get mad, I walk away because I don't want to deal with it anymore. Kaye has helped me because she has told me that it's not a good attitude. I need to continue dialoguing so we can get to the real issue. How are we going to address this in a civilized manner so we can express our needs and desires? We have to try to come to an adult conclusion without losing our tempers and yelling. I want to communicate so Kaye knows what I'm feeling and thinking.

Kaye:

When you are in a relationship with someone you love and you trust, you respect their opinions. You know their opinions won't always be the same as yours. If you have been in a relationship where your opinions have not been respected, but belittled, you've heard "I can't believe anybody would..." or "I thought you of all people would know better than that." But if you are in an open and honest relationship, you can trust that it is okay to share your opinion.

In the past, Rich would go into his turtle mode. He would take everything into his shell. I would have to tap to get him to come out and talk. As I see Rich is coming out of his shell, I see him staying in the conversation because he now knows that he can trust me. I'm glad we don't always have the same opinion and I say, "Thank goodness." Now we continue talking about anything without putting each other down.

Question: Kaye, as someone who loves, respects, and wants to protect Rich's manhood, how did you express to him that you needed him to communicate more with you? Was it a one-time discussion or was it a process?

Kaye:

Oh no, it was *definitely* a process. When Rich would not communicate with me, that was a form of control. You are controlling the environment whether you realize it or not. You're shutting a person down when you're not staying in there. I cried a lot and Rich saw that. I went to another place in the house away from him. Then I shut myself down and asked God for more skills in order to be able to communicate with him.

Rich would come in, realizing for whatever reason I was really hurt. I remember six or seven years ago he came in and said, "What can I do?" I was touched by that and asked if he could just hold me. He did and just let me cry. Later, I could tell him, "I need to know more about how you are feeling." I said that he needed to train me how to treat him just like I needed to train him how to treat me. When he shuts down I don't know what to do. Sometimes the most intimate moments are when we are silent, either holding hands or each other. That's how we started, so we remember those moments. We build on them. Rich always comes back and says, "What can I do?"

Rich:

It goes back to the differences between men and women, with the male typically more logical than the female. What Kaye was saying here is that something may happen and I'm sitting here thinking, "I don't understand." Men call it a gut feeling, women call it their intuition; you know something is wrong but you don't know what. So you ask. You say, "What?" That's something I try to pick up more on and go find out what is wrong.

Question: How long did your previous marriage last?

Kaye:

28 years.

Rich:

The first one was 16 years and the second was 4 years.

Question: This longevity demonstrates your credibility and shows you were not just in and out of relationships. What made you realize you wanted to get married again and were there fears about doing that again?

Kaye:

After my divorce, and I take marriage very seriously, it broke my heart. I had to become that person I was looking for. I wrote down everything I wanted to establish about myself. I spent eight years working on myself. I took courses, went to counseling, traveled, looked at marriages that were working. I went back to school, earning my graduate degree in special education and started my new profession. I became the person I hopefully wanted to find: Somebody who had empathy, and vision for this marriage of honesty and integrity and love. I wanted a companion that I could trust and enjoy the rest of my life with. Someone with whom I could blend families and create joy.

After eight years of that, I thought, "Now I don't really need anybody, but I want somebody." I didn't need Rich, but I knew he would help fill a gap in my life to share his life, children and grandchild with. I felt blessed, but I knew it would be a lot of work because at our age and stage of life, we have a tremendous backpack of experiences.

We tend to see a new relationship through the lenses of our past experiences and we both had that. Many of them were dysfunctional and I was a part of that dysfunction. I had to change my paradigm of thinking and my own behaviors. I learned lots of new skills and I am continuing to learn because I believe it is a lifelong process.

Question: Without defining them, will you list some of the new skills you learned in those eight years?

Kaye:

Listening, learning empathy, respecting other peoples' positions, understanding others have made mistakes (we are all human), we are all here to share this wonderful like together. I also learned to become *proactive* and not *reactive* in my life. I learned to set boundaries for people and be able to say, 'No.' I stopped being the people pleaser and peacemaker, which takes a lot of courage. You have to risk a lot to be able to say to someone that you can't accept their behavior.

Question: Did you have any fear about going into a third marriage, and if so, how did you overcome it?

Rich:

I didn't have any, really. It was a process. I didn't go into it with the answers. It just felt right. (Now I've switched the tables on the women typically being the intuitive one and the male being the logical one.) I can't say that I did think it through; it just seemed right. I did know I was embarking on a journey and that I had no idea where it was going. Now that I'm in it, I remember what you told us about 2 ½ years ago: We are supposed to work at it and make it work.

When we disagree, I have to step back and think how do I change my behavior to make this better. I don't mean that I'm broken and Kaye needs to fix me, just that I need to be more open to how she is feeling or why she is saying or doing something. It's a new experience. You arrive at a point and say, "Gee, I've never been here before, what do I do?" So it's a learning process. I didn't enter with fear, knowing it is a process.

This has been the one time where I'm really trying to make it work instead of saying, "Well, phooey, this is not working, I'm out of here." I had a good friend who said every time he gets a divorce, it gets easier and easier. He was on his third divorce when he made that comment. I don't want to make it easier; I want to make it work! So when we don't know what to do, we talk about it.

Kaye:

We dated for five years. He relied a lot on the opinions of his daughters, sister and brother-in-law and other friends. The more we were with friends and family, the more we became comfortable with thinking of being married. I told Rich I wanted to show our respect for each other by being married with a commitment, which was important to me. But we worked for five years on this. I remember an occasion when Rich's daughter said, "Dad, she's a real keeper, don't let her get away." I thought, "Wow, that is such a wonderful validation of our love!"

Question: So you had some input from people you love and trust for confirmation of this marriage?

Both:

> Yes

Question: What do you two do to continue being good friends?

Rich:

> We enjoy similar things, reading, tennis, skiing. Kaye has a musical background and I enjoy going to the plays. I believe in trying to maintain those things you enjoyed before you were married and continue to enjoy them together. We struggle with time because our work, our distance from our jobs, places a tremendous demand on our time with each other. It is easy to run out of time, which puts a strain on the fun part of life and saying, "Let's go play tennis." We have to really schedule these things into our lives.

Kaye:

> I think you have to be able to laugh together, making little things fun. We spend two times a week doing things together. We ski at least once a year. We go to Palm Springs, once a year to play tennis with friends. We maintain a lot of activities, which is crucial. We do have to plan ahead. We golf. We go to one or two Broncos games a year.
>
> Rich does a great job of planning. Rich does incredible things for me for no special reason, demonstrating his love for me. I can come home and see flowers. Once he bought a Happy Meal. I wanted something to eat but I

didn't want a McDonald's. He bought be a Happy Meal because it had a funny little guy in it. I kept him and call him "Jose Happy." He still sits in my car. I've had him for seven months. I laugh when I get in the car. It reminds me of Rich's love   for me.

Rich leaves me sticky notes all around, which say, "I love you" or "I love you still." I never know where I'm going to find them. I think this is important. You don't have to have a fight to do this. Rich will sometimes make me cookies. Keep the fun things going and laugh.

Question: What role does or did God play in your marriage?

Kaye:

I can speak for me. God has always been my guidance always. What I do, I just talk to Him and ask Him to send me a sign or send me an angel. It is a personal thing that I do. God always tells me not to be afraid, I'm watching over you, and that I can trust Rich, and you can open up to him, because I don't always. He is love and says "'Fear not." I believe He sends birds and squirrels around the house to make me laugh. The squirrels scatter the birds and it reminds me to be playful. Rich and I do not read the Bible together. And before I moved to this city, I never missed church or choir and I need to put that back into my life. Hopefully, I will.

Rich:

I look at it from an intellectual, logical perspective. I believe that we are all part of the whole. If I get to feeling a little blue, I remind myself that we are all to-gether. From a God perspective, I see God as the whole

thing. In the Bible, it says that God is all-knowing, everywhere, all-powerful and for God to be that, He must be
everything. I am part of that, I have a right to be here,
and we are all equal. I like to feel that I'm among a
Presence. No one can take my soul.

Question: What suggestions would make to a divorced person
who desires to remarry?

Rich:

    Kaye has taught me to communicate and to be sensi-
tive to the other person's needs, wishes, desires. Sometimes you can sense the other person has a problem even
if she doesn't express it. So I ask, 'Did I do something
wrong?' And it may not be your fault, but you can try to
help, by asking, "Should I leave you alone or hold you?"
You need the willingness to take the next step beyond
instead of saying, "I'm out of here."

Kaye:

    I think it is crucial that you know where you are going.
You are on this journey and need a map for direction.
What are your common goals in life? What do you
visualize this relationship to be? Do you wanted to be
surrounded with joy, friends, family, blended family. Is
your profession going to be number one? I think your
relationship has to be first priority. And you must determine that ahead of time, before the wedding.

    Quite frankly, people at our stage of life have their
profession or their sports, golf, or hobby and that's their
number one love; then their spouse and friends are their

second or third. You are not in the relationship to change the other person. You are there to enjoy them. You shouldn't go into a relationship saying, "When he's with me, he will be this way." Love, respect, honesty, openness, and communication are important to me.

We wanted to be surrounded by the love of our relationship first and then be surrounded by our blended family and friends. I knew by Rich's family, friends, that he was solid. I knew that I never was going to have to try to change that. It starts with a strong foundation. And if a person doesn't have a social conscious and you see them lying and cheating, these are their patterns of behavior and you are not going to change them. Some people want materialism. Create the joy you want.

Question: What did you like about the HomeBuilders? (This is a FamilyLife.com, Bible-based group study for couples. We had five couples in our group).

Kaye:

There were a couple of things that I liked about it. Number one, the study made you sit down and do it because you knew that you were going to be meeting, you couldn't put it off because there were Scriptures to read and talk about. You had to put it in your schedule, which I thought was awesome. I would do it again for that purpose.

I love relating Scriptures to real life. I loved the fellowship of the group because everybody seemed to be so open and honest. It was reassuring to realize that everyone has issues, or weaknesses and strengths in their relationships. It was fun being able to laugh and share.

And I really felt lonely when the study ended because I thought, 'Wow, I'm not going to see these people and I looked forward to each study time together, discussing the Scriptures in relation to our marriages. I liked the diversity of the group, in ages, newlyweds, "old weds," race, everything.

Question: What didn't you like about it?

Kaye:

> I can't think of anything.

Question: What could be done to improve it?

Kaye:

> With that particular group, I'm not sure anything could be done to improve it.

Rich:

> I enjoyed it too. I liked meeting every two weeks. I think weekly would be too much because of my schedule. I would like to do it with other couples. It was nice to see couples wrestling with similar issues.

Kaye:

> Marriage has potential for conflict: (1) disciplining children; (2) finances-having common goals there; (3) how you spend your leisure time from both points of view. As a stay-at-home mom for twenty years, I didn't set any boundaries and eventually felt used. How can you create joy in marriage? The key is balance, which is why I think it is important to be in a group that is trying to

balance their relationship. I think people need to be grateful, that we are here and being watched over. I try to ask this during the day: "Kaye, what are you grateful for today?" I have a daily opportunity to get by the thorns on the rose bush, so I can get to the roses.

Larry & Renetta

Larry and Renetta are the second couple interviewed. They have been married nine years. This is Larry's third marriage and Renetta's first. Here's their interview:

Question: Larry, what are some things you plan to do differently to make this your last marriage?

Larry:

Realize that no one is perfect, and understand some things about myself: things that set well with me, and things that set me off. I didn't expect someone who was my companion for life to be deceitful or misleading. You wonder how far a lie went and how deep into the marriage it went.

Question: Larry, how do you work through the trust factor in order to go into another marriage relationship? Was there some point you had to trust her and become vulnerable again or did you just step out there by faith or was it a process?

Larry:

It was not a preconceived process. I had to trust what was in my heart but at the same time, trust what was in my mind too. For example, her sensitivity to her cats helped me see that she's a warm and caring person and tends to give people more chances. That let me know what kind of person she was.

Question: So her character was a big plus; you got to see her in action.

Larry:

It was like I planned that the relationship wouldn't go any further until I saw that God was directing the whole thing. And the whole distaste I had for dishonesty, she felt the same way. It just came up in a discussion.

Question: Renetta, you were getting ready to marry a man who had already been married two times before. What were you thinking as to how, for you, this was going to be the last marriage for both of you?

Renetta:

I didn't feel that way immediately. I was thinking to myself, "What was the longest marriage he had?" Five years. So I wondered if I could make it five years. What would he feel for me after five years? I was worried because I was his third wife. Was I going to keep his interest? What is different about me that would make him want to stay?

Through our dating, engagement, and first three years of marriage, I was not real secure. One good thing about our dating was that we were best friends. When he asked me to marry him I was of course excited. We had never argued but after we were engaged, we started arguing all the time. I wondered what was going on. We were better friends before getting engaged! His friendship was more

important than being married, so after a week of arguing
I took my "Yes" back!

Question: Why do you think you started arguing after you first
got engaged?

Larry:

I'll tell you, it had to do with my first two marriages. I
started thinking "Oh man, I'm getting ready to get
married again!" The first two didn't work out and it was
tough. It took a long time to get over. I was comfortable
with where I was, but at the same time I didn't think I
would get married again. But she changed my mind and
heart about that. I begin to get apprehensive, scared, and
wondered, "What if it ends the same way as the others?"
I didn't think I could handle that again. It took so much
out of me the first two times.

Question: So there was a little insecurity and fear?

Larry:

Yep.

Renetta:

A *lot* of fear insecurity and fear! He was so fearful that
if friends invited him to a wedding he was cool and
collected outside of the church, but as soon as he went
inside he'd break out in a sweat.

Larry:

Yep, I really would. And I'd get this cold chill down
the middle of my back and start perspiring.

Clarence:

OK. I'm interviewing two other couples. One has been married maybe 3 years. It's the second marriage for her and his third. For the third couple in Chicago it's the second for both of them. How long have you been married?

Larry:

The 31st of this month it will be 9 years.

Renetta:

Whoohoo!!

Clarence:

That's great!

Renetta:

Yo baby!

Larry:

And it's great! We still like to laugh and have fun. God has blessed us with that. We really believe He brought us together and we wouldn't be the people we are now without the experiences we went through previously. We've learned that appreciation for each other and that friendship is very important.

Question: You keep mentioning periodically about your faith. What role did that play for you, Larry, were you a follower of Jesus Christ before you met Renetta?

Larry:

Yes.

Question: How has you faith changed since you have met and been married to her?

Larry:

> I would say it has gotten even closer and developed in that one-on-one relationship with Christ. I had that before but my faith has grown. I trust even more, even in aspects that I didn't even think about before.

Question: In your previous marriages and/or relationships did you pray together?

Larry:

> In my first one we did but in the second one we didn't.

Renetta:

> And I wasn't married but had a dating relationship for about nine years and we didn't pray together.

Question: How did it feel when you went past the five year milestone?

Renetta:

> For me it's been really fun. We make each other laugh and get to know each other. There are still little surprises that pop up when you least expect it. God is so amazing because He gives us each a role and sometimes we switch roles. Right now, I'm acting like he was last year and I'm like he was. It's never the same but it's comfortable and I'm very secure in knowing that we love each other, he loves me and we trust each other. That's the biggest thing; our trust has just grown.

You think you've reached a level of friendship and that level just keeps heightening. Life keeps putting obstacles in you path anyway and as a married couple you grow to expect (a mutual expectancy) that your spouse is going to be there for you. Together, we have a better chance of overcoming the obstacles.

Sometimes, I wake Larry up from a dead sleep at three a.m. and tell him I love him. He says "I love you too" and we just hold hands and go back to sleep. Sometimes I wake him up because I need to talk and we talk for hours.

Larry:

Yep. You can't put everything on a time schedule. You gotta have some unexpected things that occur and you still be able to reach out to one another. Even though you are doing life together, so to speak, you still have different aspects that affect each one of us different. A key point is really truly being friends. When you have a friend, they don't always come to you when everything is great. Sometimes they just need you to listen when things bother them. You may not be able to solve their problem but it helps them to know that you care enough to listen, talk to them and give feedback.

Renetta:

If they want it.

Larry:

Yeah, you know if they want it or not, to be able to converse with them. It's very important. As a guy with a best friend, if that person needs something, I may or may not have it, but I'm going to try to be there for them. I'm not going to kick them to the curb or leave them stranded. I want them to know that hey, they can call on me and if I can, I'm going to definitely help them. I want her to feel the same thing because she's my friend and I want her to know that!

Clarence:

It sounds like you guys really are best friends. You hold hands, make each other laugh, confide in each other, and date. Is there anything you haven't mentioned that you do to keep each other as best friends? What would you tell a newlywed couple to do to stay best friends?

Larry:

In today's society things are fast paced. You always have things pulling at you from different directions. Make sure you keep time for each other to do things you like doing. You may have long schedules or long weeks, but you have to slip time in for yourselves. It might mean losing a little sleep or not watching that fantastic game that you want to see, but it's important that you don't lose that time with each other so you can keep that friendship.

Renetta:

And I would say a really important thing is that we are not perfect, and will not always get along or always see eye to eye, but it is important that when those particular situations come up that we respect each other's barriers and boundaries.

Number one, like my mom used to always tell us, "Don't go to sleep mad." That's just so hard to do or to not do because when you're mad it's like, "I don't want to talk to you. We have nothing else to say." You'll go your own separate ways. He goes in the living room and sits in the Lazy Boy and I go into the bedroom. We're both mad, we're not talking to each other and we're feeling terrible. And then I'm like "Ooh, I'm not going to be first (laugh)." And I go, "Ooh honey, I'm sorry." And he'll say, "Honey, I'm sorry." So it doesn't matter who said it first.

Larry:

It doesn't matter who said it first or who said it last.

Renetta:

Right. We don't keep tabs on each other. It's just humbling, because once you can break those walls down and you can drop that barrier, then you are actually able to talk.

Larry:

I'd like to add that because we are different individuals, you discover that different things really upset your partner. It may have something to do with their upbringing or adulthood, but whatever it is, once you find out that's something you want to tread softly around. When you get angry or upset, don't push those buttons. Stay away from pushing those buttons.

Question: Renetta, you said something about respecting each other's boundaries? What do you mean by that?

Renetta:

Okay, let's say we just had a disagreement about HANGING MY CHRISTMAS LIGHTS! I want my Christmas lights to be hung! I'm the driving kind: "Come on, we can do it, let's get them done!" Larry is more laid back and says, "We'll get to it. Don't worry about it, it's not Christmas yet."

I want them up so I can look at them for a few weeks. Larry thinks if we get them up the day before Christmas, we're doing good. That causes tension and conflict because I'm not getting what I want. I'm pushing and Larry is not getting what he wants. After a point we have to understand each other. I have to back off and say, "I can't put the lights on the roof by myself." The only person who can do that is Larry. I have to respect how he feels and ask, "Is it really that important to get them up right now? But it *is* important to get them up sooner than Christmas Eve, so is there anything I can do to get him to compromise with me?"

The more I press, the more he backs into a corner and won't want to put them up at all. We've learned it's a button and we have to find out why we are that way. He has a sensitivity. He works every other weekend. I have every one off. I'm free and clear, he wants to relax on the few weekends he has off. I have to respect what feeds into why he reacts the way he does and back off. If it gets to a point we have tension in the air, like we did with the lights, I'm going to back off.

One day I called him and he was getting ready to put them up. He got a neighbor to help and did it. He didn't want me to be upset with him for not doing it. I assured him I wouldn't be. He said he had to remember that the little kid in me comes out when I see the lights because we didn't have them growing up. He has to realize that is important to me. Therefore, it has to be important to him also.

Jerald & Jerra

My third couple has been married for more than 18 years. They are dear friends of mine and consented to this interview, hoping that sharing what they have learned and are learning will be helpful to those of you reading this chapter. He is the pastor and she is the first lady of one of fastest growing churches in one of America's largest cities.

Question: What was or were your fears entering into a second marriage and what did you do to overcome them?

Jerald:

It was my second marriage and Jerra's first. My greatest fear was a repeat of the first one. I believe I was called to be a husband and father, you know the whole deal. I think I was afraid because I planned to wait at least ten years before considering remarriage because of my divorce. The first marriage was so messed up and I didn't want to do that again. I didn't overcome the fear right away. I think that God's love and our love was more powerful than my fear.

Question: Did your children have any concerns or fears?

Jerra:

Craig was five or six years old. His concern was whether or not I would be able to love more than one person. He was afraid of sharing my time and love with someone else. To ease that, Craig was not made to call Jerald "Dad." At first, he called him Jerald for a few years, then as their relationship developed, he called him "Daddy Jerald". Later it was just Dad.

Jerald:

My three children lived with their mom and they had a **who-o-o-le** lot of problems. They thought that Jerra was the reason that their mother and I weren'tgetting back together. They lived 1,200 miles from us. Anything they heard about Jerra was through their mother or grandmother, so there were a lot of years of problems. I think there are still a few now but they are grown and pretty okay with it.

Jerra:

Before I was considered the person you were going to marry, his children liked me. That year or so they were living here, I would do things with the older ones and they called me "Jeremiah, full of fire" (laugh), they *did* like me. As long as I was not the person he was going to marry!

Question: Did you bring any baggage into the relationship?

Jerra:

Whooahh!

Jerald:

Yeah, she brought a whole lot! We're still unloading some of her dirty laundry.

Jerra:

(laughs)

Jerald:

I brought some, she brought some. Mine was obviously from the previous marriage. My ex-wife was somewhat violent. I had a great mistrust, not so much of Jerra, but just of what was going on around me when I was asleep.

Jerra:

Yeah, trust was the biggest thing that spread out to different areas. It was trust for me too. We trusted each other to a certain extent, but when you get married, that trust has to be huge. It can't be when you say a buzz word you expect that they are going to respond a certain way. It was that way in the beginning. But we made a conscious effort to work through the trust or rather the lack thereof.

Question: What were some areas of trust you wrestled with during the first few years?

Jerald:

We've already talked about that. Her family didn't trust me *at all*. We are wonderful friends now but then I was all of the bad people you can think of wrapped into one as far as they were concerned! As they began to trust me, it got easier for Jerra.

Question: When did you begin to feel safe in this marriage?

Jerrra:

Since it was my first marriage, I did the counting deal. How many years was he married before in comparison? As I begin to seek after God with "Help me, please," and God saw that I really meant it, God began to show me things to do and not to do; buzz words and things not to say. We had a lot of all-night sessions where we talked things out and laid things out on the table, not to be hurtful but to be helpful. The more of those we had, the more it started to smooth things out.

Jerald:

I think that's true. Jerra accepted me the way I was. My first wife wanted to change me.

Question: What has helped your marriage to last so long?

Jerra:

We talk. We over-communicate. We are as one.

Jerald:

Yeah, communication is the biggest thing with us.

Jerra:

And we like each other!

Question: How did you handle conflict during the first few years and do you do it differently now?

Jerald:

In the first years, you had to explain everything. **Everything!** Now it's more of a look. We know each other so well, there are some things I know she is not going to agree with and vice versa. We're cool with that. I have to decide that it's not worth fighting over. It's not worth divorce or her going to jail. Jerra, put the knife down (laugh). That comes from communication as well. We know everything is not going to be perfect.

Jerra:

In the beginning years, someone would just leave the premises until one cooled down. Then we would talk about it.

Question: How did you deal with accepting your spouse's children?

Jerald:

I had to deal with it more than she did. My kids were 1,200 miles away and hers were in the next room. It was difficult at first. I had to deal with guilt because my son was living in a trailer park and her son was eating chicken from my table. It was hard but I knew it was a package deal and it wasn't his fault.

Jerra:

It was especially hard because at that time Craig was a special needs child with serious issues. (Much different from the way he is today.) We had to work through how to handle him and deal with all of our other issues at the same time. We had to work together as a team.

Question: What would you say to a couple thinking of entering a second or third marriage?

Jerra:

Reality check: are there children? Be careful of comparisons. Realize this is a totally different person and I have to deal with them totally different.

Jerald:

> They should get serious counseling that is going to bring out as much as possible. If you are afraid of that, it should be a red flag. People are good at hiding their own issues. They want to talk about their ex's but not about themselves. You have to get it out.

Question: What would you say to those already in their second or third marriage?

Jerald:

> If you can, communicate and over-communicate. That's the most important thing.

Jerra:

> You need to know a little bit of the history because it will help you understand why they react the way they do. What kind of upbringing did they have? When people divorce, it's usually not one person's fault so what was their part, even though it may be a one-sided explanation?

Question: What role did God play in this marriage?

Jerald:

> I didn't want to get remarried right away. I think that even though there are some things we should have done differently, God allowed us to be soul mates. Even with our age difference of five-and-a-half years.

Question: Do you pray together?

Jerald:

>Yes.

Question: How often?

Jerald:

>We don't have a set time. We just sit and do it. At first, you feel like you have to have a set program, but the longer you are together it becomes part of what you do. Maybe she thinks it's not enough.

Jerra:

>It's when we know it's really needed. I always pray for him and I know he prays for me. When we are having a tough day, it's time to pray.

Question: Has being a minister/pastor made any difference being in a second marriage?

Jerald:

>I've always been a minister. Even in my first marriage I was a young minister. I've only been a pastor for five years.

Jerra:

>Now, as he tells his story, it helps other people and lets them know they are not alone. Other people question his qualifications, but he has always been up front and open about his previous marriage.

Jerald:

>Pastoring *is* harder on the marriage. You have to share

the time. You must be so intentional to make time for each other. And no matter how much time you give, it's still doesn't seem like it's enough! Hopefully, if it's a good one, you learn how to deal with it.

I hope reading about the lives of these three couples has been helpful. And you can read and reread about how they are having victories in marriages after their first ones didn't work out. Am I trying to promote divorce? Of course not! But the reality is that some marriages don't last, and I desire to help those in second marriages as well as those in their first marriages make them your last marriage.

I have some questions that I want you to answer as an individual or with your spouse. Answering these questions honestly won't be fun, but may save your present marriage.

Have You Dealt with Your Baggage? (Do You Realize You Have Baggage?)

Maybe a practical first step is to work through the baggage of your last marriage. I'm asking you some questions which you may feel are hard or even unfair questions. But I believe that if you want your present marriage to be your last one, you must answer these questions. Please remember, I'm on the side of making your marriage your last one. So as you work through these questions by yourself, with your spouse or trusted friends, you may think that I'm your enemy, but I'm not.

Objectivity may be difficult if not impossible to maintain, but try to determine the cause of the breakdown of your last marriage. Let's take a closer evaluation other than, "The whole thing was her fault!" What may really be helpful is if you have trusted friends who love you enough to tell you the truth, even if they disagree with you. Try to be honest with yourself and them. Get two or three of them together and walk back through your last marriage.

Questions to Answer:

(1) What were some of the first warning signs that your marriage was in trouble? Did you see them? If you saw them, why did you ignore them? Did your friends see them and tell you? If they did, why did you ignore them? Did your friends see the early warning signs and not say anything to you? If this was the case, why did they do that?

(2) Did these initial warning signs continue through the duration of your last marriage? Why didn't you do something about them? Why couldn't you do something about them?

(3) What were your contributions to the breakdown of your last marriage? Why did you do what you did? If you say you didn't do anything wrong, you are lying to yourself and probably lied to your former spouse. Was it because of how you were raised by your parent (s), other relatives, foster home, etc.?

(4) Were you abused mentally or sexually as a child? Have you ever been emotionally healed from this pain or have you internalized it all of these years? (Do you know that any kind of abuse scars you emotionally, and that these scars seldom heal themselves? Therefore, they stay with you until you deal with them.)

(5) Do you have the fear of success, so you purposely sabotage a good relationship? Have you been in so many unsuccessful relationships that you feel you don't deserve to be in a mutually beneficial one? Have you been in enough unsuccessful relationships that you feel none will ever work out? Do you feel that something is wrong with you?

(6) Did you try to protect yourself and your new relationship from issues that negatively impacted your previous relationship? For example, if the issue was money, did you decide that you and your spouse will have separate financial accounts and never shall the two meet? If this was or is the case, you may not have financial problems, but it becomes difficult to build intimacy. The separate accounts symbolize the lack of trust in the couple. The couple is saying intentionally or unintentionally, "I love you, BUT! This is as close as you get!" In order for your spouse and your relationship to make your dreams a reality, you must give your spouse the opportunity to fail. The same channel used for failure is the same one used for success. This requires vulnerability. This why biblical pre-marital counseling is so crucial to the success of a marriage.

(7) Do you keep your commitments? Do you have a set limit as to how much of anything you are going to take off your spouse? Does your spouse know that you have these limitations? Why or why not?

(8) What did you learn from your previous relationship about you that is good and what you need to work on?

These are just a few questions you need to consider. Once you work through these, you and/or your friends can think of others which may be necessary for your specific situation.

What Will Be Different This Next Time Around?

Now, that you are into a new marriage, what is going to be different? I know you have a new spouse, but ....*what guarantees do you have that this marriage will be different?*

You may need a better plan than that you are going to work harder. What will you do differently in order to make this marriage your last one? What baggage from your last marriage do you need to leave and is there any you need to bring into this new relationship?

What Are Your Plans to Make This Marriage Your Last One?

Do you have any plans to make this marriage your last one? Your actions and your attitude may need to change. How so? Your attitude toward divorce may need to become that, for you, divorce is not an option.

Do You Have an Accountability Partner?

Most of our lives, we find ourselves in some form of accountability: at work, school, as a child, as a parent.

I have often asked older married men to hold me accountable in the way that I treat Brenda. It has proved to be a blessing to have someone with experience about how to be a better husband to ask, "What did you do when this happened?" It is also good to know that what I share with Bob Cook or Michael Jones stays confidential.

I realize this chapter probably brought up some old painful memories. Remember, that the purpose of this chapter isn't to reopen old wounds, but to save you from future unnecessary wounds. So let me encourage you to work through the pain of your past because it may save your present, your future, and the family.

There is no judgment here, but simply a friend who wants to help. Here's to making this your last marriage!

Action Points
Chapter Ten
Making This Your Last Marriage

1. If you are single (divorced) and desire to remarry, re-evaluate your last marriage and what went wrong.

2. Be honest, because if you aren't you may repeat your mistakes. How did you contribute to the demise of your last marriage?

3. How are you disciplining yourself not to repeat your mistakes?

For Your Pastor:
1. Dear Pastor, please help your singles (never been married and divorcees)and marrieds by preaching on marriage at least seven times a year.

2. Get your church to begin praying for the singles (high school, college, and on up) in your church for them to understand that if they are followers of Christ, that they are complete. They don't have to be married to be complete. And if they want to get married, pray for them to not settle for less than God's Best!

3. Pray for the protection and health of your married couples.

4. Encourage all couples in your church, especially leadership (paid and volunteer) to attend or hold a marriage seminar yearly and you set the example by attending yourself with your spouse (if you are married).